theocracy

theocracy

LILA PERL

Marshall Cavendish
Benchmark
New York

Marshall Cavendish Benchmark
99 White Plains Road • Tarrytown, NY
10591 • www.marshallcavendish.us •
Copyright © 2008 by Marshall Cavendish
Corporation • Maps Copyright © 2008 by
Marshall Cavendish Corporation • Maps by
XNR Productions, Inc. • All rights reserved.
No part of this book may be reproduced or
utilized in any form or by any means electro-
nic or mechanical including photocopying,
recording, or by any information storage and
retrieval system, without permission from the
copyright holders. • All Internet sites were
available and accurate when sent to press. •
Library of Congress Cataloging-in-Publication
Data • Perl, Lila. • Theocracy / Lila Perl. •
v. cm.—(Political systems of the world) •
Summary: "Gives an overview of theocracy
as a political system, including an historical
discussion of theocratic regimes throughout the world"—Provided by publisher. •
Includes bibliographical references and index. •
Contents: Iran today : an Islamic theocracy—
The ancient world : an Egyptian theocracy—
Mesoamerican theocracies : the Maya and the
Aztecs—A Christian theocracy : Mormons in
the young United States—A Taliban theocracy:
Afghanistan in the 1990s—Could religious
fundamentalism lead to future theocracies? •
ISBN-13: 978-0-7614-2631-8 • 1. Theocracy—
Juvenile literature. I. Title. • JC372.P385 2007 •
321'.5—dc22 2006026055 • Photo research by
Connie Gardner • Cover photo by Michael
S. Yamashita/CORBIS • Photographs in the
book are used by permission and through the
courtesy of: *Corbis*: Ramin Talaie, back cover,
1, 3; Abedin Taherkenareh/epa, 41; Arte and
Immagini sri, 74; Bettmann, 79; Desmond
Boylan, 98; Gil Cohen Mage, 121; Mona
Sharaf/Reuters, 124; *Getty Images*: AFP, 11, 95;
Time Life Pictures, 24, 68; Getty Image News,
126; *AP Photo*: Hasan Sarbakhshian, 37; Michel
Euler, 111; The Granger Collection: 53, 65, 81.
Publisher: Michelle Bisson • Art Director:
Anahid Hamparian • Series Designer: Sonia
Chaghatzbanian • Printed in Malaysia
1 3 5 6 4 2

WITH THANKS TO EUGENE V.
GALLAGHER, ROSEMARY PARK
PROFESSOR OF RELIGIOUS STUDIES
FACULTY FELLOW, CENTER
FOR TEACHING AND LEARNING,
CONNECTICUT COLLEGE, FOR
HIS EXPERT REVIEW OF THIS
MANUSCRIPT.

Contents

theocracy

Foreword ■ ■

IT IS NOVEMBER 1979 and the scene is the United States Embassy compound in Tehran, capital of the Middle Eastern nation of Iran.

The compound, comprising one of the largest diplomatic outposts in the world, sprawls over roughly twenty-seven acres or about twenty-five city blocks and resembles a small city. Among its structures are the two-story embassy building, a separate consulate, the elegant residence of the American ambassador, a military barracks, a warehouse, a motor pool, a co-op store, and even a ten-story apartment building to serve as additional living quarters and to house visitors. All of the foregoing is laid out on gracefully landscaped grounds, with manicured lawns, winding paths, and shade trees. Surrounding the entire compound is a mile-long wall that is as high as twelve feet in some places. Heavy metal gates guard the entrances to the compound.

Beyond the walls of the embassy compound lies downtown Tehran, a bustling metropolis of five million. Since the early1940s, Iran had been under the rule of a royal figure known as Mohammad Reza Shah Pahlavi, or simply the Shah. Enormously wealthy and with strong leanings toward the West, the Shah had been on good terms with the United States for many years.

Up until recently, the Iranian capital reflected the influence of the Shah's modernization of his ancient land, which had been converted to the religion of Islam in the 600s CE. Fashionable European shops and gleaming office towers contrasted sharply with domed mosques and with slum neighborhoods of ramshackle tin-roofed dwellings and smoky factory districts. Western dress, movies, music, and television were in evidence in Tehran, and even in other cities around the country, although much less so in rural areas, where traditional Islam frowned on them.

Since January 16, 1979, however, vast changes have come about in Iran. On that date, following many months of protest against the Shah and his government by powerful Muslim clerics and by student demonstrators, Mohammad Reza Shah Pahlavi left the country. Announcing that he was going abroad for a short holiday, and accompanied by his wife and a full entourage, the monarch, who had occupied the so-called Peacock Throne for thirty-seven years, took off for Egypt.

His exile—for that, in fact, was what it was—soon took him from there to Morocco, the Bahamas, Mexico, and, on October 22, 1979, to the United States. Technically the Shah, who was suffering from lymphoma (cancer of the lymph glands), was admitted to New York Hospital for medical treatment and not for the purpose of taking refuge in the United States. But the reaction of the Islamic revolutionary movement at home in Iran was to prove fateful. It would have a marked effect on the reelection campaign and political future of President Jimmy Carter of the United States and a shattering impact on the United States Embassy and scores of embassy personnel in Tehran.

"Death to America!" "Death to the Shah!" "Death to Carter!" These were the cries of some 450 to 500 student demonstrators who gathered outside the gates of the embassy compound at 7:30 on the morning of Sunday, November 4, 1979. The men and women working at the embassy were not, however, overly alarmed. For such chanting had been common for about two weeks now, ever since the Shah had entered the United States for cancer treatment on October 22.

Who were the Iranian students? Mainly they were from various colleges and from Tehran's Polytechnic University. They were young Islamic revolutionaries, who had allied themselves with Muslim religious leaders advocating turning away from the Western influences introduced by the Shah and a return to the fundamentalist teachings of the Koran, the Muslim holy book.

The Ayatollah Ruhollah Khomeini (left) was the driving force behind Iran's religious revolution of 1979.

Most influential of the members of the Muslim clergy in Iran was the Ayatollah Ruhollah Khomeini (*ayatollah* is the title given to the most learned and pious of Iran's religious leaders). Even though Khomeini had been arrested for religious radicalism and then banished from Iran by the Shah in 1964, his power had grown during his absence of thirteen years, most of which he had spent in Iraq. In 1978, Khomeini was expelled from Iraq and went to live in France, a base from which he was able to issue his revolutionary message even more strongly. On February 1, 1979, only two weeks after the Shah had gone into exile, leaving behind him a weak provisional government, Khomeini returned to Iran from his years of exile.

The Islamic revolutionary students rallied to his cause. Their complaints against the Shah were numerous. He had suppressed their secret societies and had spied on them through his brutal secret police force known as SAVAK, notorious for administering physical torture. The word SAVAK is an acronym (derived from the first letters) of the Persian "Organization for Intelligence and National Security." Like Khomeini and Iran's other religious leaders, the student zealots saw the Shah's international business dealings with the United States and other Western nations as a betrayal of Iranian nationalism and the rape of the country's natural resources, including its oil. For the principal beneficiaries of the Shah's willingness to accept what appeared to the students as foreign domination and economic exploitation were the Shah, his family, and his cronies. Most of all, the students regarded the Shah as anti-Islamic and the enemy of their religion and all that it stood for.

Both men and women made up the ranks of the militant students who had been appearing outside the walls of the embassy compound for many mornings now. The young men were bearded in the orthodox Islamic fashion. The young women wore dark head shawls that covered their hair and long black garments in keeping with the Islamic demand for modesty in female dress. The militants were probably best described as revolutionary reactionaries, fighting for changes that would undo any progressive moves toward secular education and female equality that had been instituted by the Shah.

Who, however, would have dreamed that on that Sunday—November 4, 1979—an ordinary working day on the Islamic calendar, a loose throng of some 450 student demonstrators would be so fired up with passion for their cause and anti-American rage that they would successfully storm the United States Embassy?

"I remember standing in a window and looking down on all the noise and anti-American anger," said Moorhead C. Kennedy Jr., one of the mission's highest-ranking diplomats, as he watched the threatening mob approach the walls of the compound. "And I wondered to myself what it would be like to die."

The protesters carried clubs and sticks, and large posters mounted on poles, of the Ayatollah Ruhollah Khomeini. Only a relatively small number, it would later be revealed, carried knives or guns. Yet, within hours they had climbed the main gates and scaled the twelve-foot walls of the compound in a number of different places.

In the melee that followed the invasion of the compound, the handful of U. S. Marine guards on hand, limiting their use of weapons to tear gas, proved unable to hold off the assault. Some members of the embassy staff were beaten with lead pipes and kicked. Others were threatened with pistols and knives. In the end, sixty-six Americans were taken prisoner and exhibited blindfolded to what now appeared to be a crowd of thousands of Iranians screaming, "God is great!" "Long live Khomeini!" and "Death to the Americans!"

The Iran hostage crisis, as the shocking event of November 4, 1979, would come to be known, resulted in fourteen and a half months, or 444 days, of captivity for a slightly whittled down group of fifty-two Americans. (Women and African Americans were released and some American males fled to the Canadian Embassy and were smuggled out of Iran.) The prisoners lived lives of deprivation, indignities, and humiliation. Many were blindfolded most of the time and tied to chairs or confined to close, dark quarters. Their relationships with their student captors varied. Some tormented the hostages almost daily with threats of death, while others simply denied them fresh air, exercise, human contact, and showers.

The experiences of the captive Americans and how each of them coped with the fears and uncertainty of their long incarceration in Iran add up to several volumes of writing on that subject alone. The hostage-taking had many other ramifications as well. It drew the attention of the United States and the rest of the world to the fact that it was witnessing the first fundamentalist Islamic revolution of modern times. A traditional monarchy of a dictatorial nature had been overthrown, and a political system known as a *theocracy*—a form of government in which the rulers are the leaders of the dominant religion and their policies are strongly influenced by that religion—was coming onto the world scene.

The word theocracy comes from the Greek for god (*theos*) and power (*kratos*). So when we speak of a theocracy, we mean a state that is governed by a divinity or by high-ranking officials who are considered to be divinely guided.

Theocratic forms of government, with rulership by godlike or god-endowed leaders, have existed on earth since earliest times, and there are many examples ranging from ancient Egypt to the partial rule of the Taliban in Afghanistan in the 1990s. Iran, however, is the prime example of a fervent contemporary theocracy that has existed since 1979. Why did this turn of events take place in Iran rather than other Islamic nations of the Middle East? How did this change come about after centuries of Iranian, also known as Persian, history? And what is life in this theocratic nation like in the twenty-first century?

1
Iran Today: AN ISLAMIC THEOCRACY ■ ■

UNTIL 1935, THE COUNTRY WE CALL IRAN TODAY was generally known in the West as Persia. Its name and national origin go back to at least 1500 BCE, when Central Asian peoples known as Persians—along with similar groups such as Medes and Scythians—began to settle the area. The earliest traces of civilization in the region, though, stem from the very beginnings of settled agricultural life, in the sixth century BCE. From that distant era, we have evidence of dwellings made of sun-dried bricks and of clay pottery.

Most famous historically is the Persian Empire of Cyrus the Great and his successors, which dominated the Middle East and beyond from 550 BCE to 330 BCE. It was Cyrus, who ascended the throne in 559 and died in 529, who conquered Babylon and liberated the captive Jews in 539 BCE. The Persian kings of Cyrus's dynasty, known as the Achaemenids, later added Egypt to their empire and, for some years, ruled an area that extended from Greece to India. The power and vastness of the Persian Empire ended, however, with its conquest by Alexander the Great in 330 BCE.

Other Persian rulers attempted to revive the empire. Prominent among them was the dynasty of the Sassanids, who ruled from 224 CE to 642 CE, and who established Zoroastrianism as the state religion.

Zoroaster, also known as Zarathustra, was an ancient Persian prophet. Although his dates are uncertain, he is believed to have

Was Persia a Theocracy under the Zoroastrian Religion?

Zoroastrianism came to be seen as a militant, or warlike, religion because it stressed the importance of overcoming the forces of evil with those of righteousness. It also considered the human body to be of such lowly material value that burying the deceased in the ground, burning the body, or drowning it were violations of the elements of earth, fire, and water. Even today, Zoroastrians, many of whom now live in India, dispose of their dead by exposing their bodies atop specially constructed towers, where they can be quickly reduced to heaps of bones by predatory birds.

During the time of Cyrus the Great and the Achaemenids, and later under the Sassanids, Zoroastrianism appears to have been the guiding light of Persia. Under the Sassanids (224 CE to 642 CE), there was an enormously powerful class of priests who directed the state religion and shared authority with the military commanders, the great landowners, and the civil administrators of the state.

Yet the overall head of state, the Sassanid emperor, was not himself a religious figure. Although he called himself "king of kings," he did not claim to be identified with or related to a deity or to possess any sort of personal divinity. His rule included the centralization of his holdings, the suppression of the power of the local lords, the administration of a far-flung system of taxation, and the maintenance of a stratified social system, including the Zoroastrian priesthood.

The word theocracy does imply unopposed rulership by a supreme leader, which was true of the Sassanid heads of state. But these rulers do not appear to have been considered gods, or to have been endowed with divine qualities, as were the priestly kings of certain other ancient civilizations or the highest level of the clergy in certain religions, such as the ayatollahs of today's Iran.

So, we cannot say that the Sassanid emperors were theocratic rulers. This political picture would change, however, with the introduction of the powerful new religion of Islam into Persia in the 600s CE.

lived around 600 BCE. His view of the spiritual world was that there was a single god who was responsible for keeping the forces of evil from subjugating those of goodness and benevolence. Zoroastrianism supplanted the earliest religion of Persia, which was probably the worship of a pantheon of nature gods. It took its place during the glory days of the Persian Empire in the 500s BCE, and may have been a strong element in the conquering zeal of Cyrus the Great and his successors.

THE ISLAMIC CONQUEST OF PERSIA

The religion known as Islam arose on the Arabian Peninsula, a desert land that lay to the southwest of the Persian Empire of the Sassanids. Its people were for the most part nomads, also known as bedouins (Arabic for desert dwellers), who had been wandering the land for centuries pasturing their sheep and goats. They used the domesticated camel for transportation as they made their way from place to place in search of pasturelands, oases, and the widely scattered towns that dotted the area.

It was in one of these mud-and-brick towns in western Arabia known as Mecca that the founder and prophet of Islam, Muhammad, was born sometime around the year 570. Little is known of his youth. It is believed that he was orphaned as a child and cared for by male relatives. On reaching his young manhood, he became a camel driver for a widow some fifteen years older than he whom he soon married.

As he advanced in years, Muhammad acquainted himself through observation and discussion with the monotheistic religions of Judaism and Christianity. Their beliefs in a single God contrasted sharply with the paganism of the Arabian peoples. In Mecca, where Muhammad lived, was the Kaaba, a cube-shaped stone building that housed 360 objects of worship of the people of Mecca and thereabouts, which Muhammad considered false gods.

In preaching against their worship and urging the local populace to accept one universal God—Allah—Muhammad put his life in danger. In 622 CE, he and his converts were forced to flee Mecca and to travel some 200 miles north to Medina, where he could continue his teaching that Allah was the one and only God and that Muhammad was his prophet.

The new religion, Islam (which is Arabic for submission to the will of God), promised rewards for those who obeyed Allah's commands and vengeance for those who did not. Islam was also a religion of reform. It promised equality for all men, generosity to the poor, and kindness to the stranger. The unifying message of Islam, as written in the Koran, Chapter 49:10, is: "Hearken, O ye men unto my words and take ye them to heart. Know ye that every Muslim is a brother unto every other Muslim, and that ye are one brotherhood."

In Medina, Muhammad's message spread with such vigor that eight years later, in 630, he made a triumphant return to Mecca where he destroyed the images of the false gods and made the Kaaba a holy place for the new religion. Islam was taken up by the peoples of Arabia and was rapidly carried far and wide in a migratory war of conquest. The Sassanids, already in a weakened state due to heavy taxation and rulers who were losing their grip on the local landholders, were easily toppled by the Arab converts to Islam. In 642, their empire collapsed.

MUHAMMAD'S SUCCESSORS AND THE RISE OF SHIA ISLAM

At the time of his death, in 632 CE, Muhammad had failed to designate a successor who would be both a spiritual leader, inheriting the mantle of Muhammad's holiness, and who would be capable of ruling as head of government over the rapidly expanding Muslim lands. Within two years of the Prophet's death, all of the Arabian Peninsula was under the influence of Islam and, by 651, the newly conquered lands of the Arabs included most of Mesopotamia (present-day Iraq), neighboring Iran, parts of Central Asia, and southern Turkey.

Who was to be designated to take on the vast responsibilities of the promising new empire? Muhammad had no direct male heir. His only living child was his daughter Fatima who was married to Ali, one of the earliest converts to the faith. In the absence of a clear directive from Muhammad making his son-in-law Ali his heir, Muhammad's followers chose one of his closest advisers to succeed him. His name was Abu Bakr, and he was to be the first of a succession of Muslim conquerors and rulers given the title of *caliph*, or successor to Muhammad.

As the wealth and success of the caliphs grew, they became increasingly elitist, making their capitals in the cities and losing direct contact with the people and with the principles of modesty and equality as taught by Muhammad and as followed through in the teachings of Ali.

Three caliphs had already succeeded Muhammad before Ali took what his followers (known as the Shia Ali, or partisans of Ali) saw as his rightful place as caliph. He established his rule in 656 at Kufa, in present-day Iraq. Ali failed, however, to gain a broad-based following among the powerful new Islamic leaders and in 661 he was assassinated

The Beliefs of Shia Islam

Shia Islam in Iran spread rapidly once the Safavid dynasty made it the official state religion in the sixteenth century, and it is today the religion of 90 percent of Iranians, as opposed to a mere 8 percent of Sunni Muslims living in Iran.

What are the principal tenets, or beliefs, of the Shia faith, and how do they compare with those of the Sunnis? The Shia Muslims observe five pillars of faith, which are shared with Sunni Muslims. They are: confession of the faith, ritual prayer, almsgiving, fasting during the daylight hours in the holy lunar month of Ramadan, and making the *hajj*, or pilgrimage, to the holy cities of Mecca and Medina at least once in one's lifetime if possible.

Differences arise, however, principally with regard to the position of Ali. While Sunni Muslims acknowledge him as the fourth of the caliphs, or successors of Muhammad, the Shiites (as Shia followers are named) revere him as the First Imam. In Shia faith, an *imam* is a major spiritual leader of great authority, who is able to interpret the mysteries of the Koran. Among Sunnis, on the other hand, the word imam is a general term for those clerics who lead prayers and offer sermons in the mosques.

A further element is the Shia belief that there were a total of twelve Imams, all of them descending from the line of Ali and his son Hussein, and culminating with the Twelfth Imam, who will one day reappear on earth as a messiah, or savior, known as the *Mahdi*.

The story of the Mahdi, whose reappearance is sought in Shia prayers and invocations (and may even be mentioned on wedding invitations), is as follows. When the Eleventh Imam died in 874, his son, who was to become the Twelfth Imam, was only five years old. Fearing for the child's life, his followers hid him from public view. The Hidden Imam, as he came to be known, remained on earth for some seventy years and then disappeared. Some believe that he never died and that when God commands it, he will manifest himself to all as the Mahdi, bringing justice and deliverance to all.

Because of the intense focus on the descent of its spiritual leaders from the line of Ali, and its fervent belief in the appearance on earth of a messiah, Shia Islam tends to concentrate both holy and political control of the state in individuals of the highest possible religious authority. The Ayatollah Khomeini, who powered the 1979 revolution that created the Islamic Republic of Iran, was one such figure. Since his death in 1989, ayatollahs of similar strength have followed him as leaders of the nation. It is this Shia belief that only a clergy with superior knowledge of the laws of God is qualified to rule their society that has resulted in the theocratic government of present-day Iran.

while at prayer in a mosque. Ali's body was buried at Najaf, also in Iraq, making Najaf one of the holiest sites for Shia Muslims—the name given to the group that was to split off from the main body known as the Sunni Muslims.

After Ali's death, an attempt was made to restore power to the family of Muhammad. Ali's youngest son, Hussein, led the Shia of southern Iraq against the army of the caliph of the new dynasty known as the Umayads. A battle took place at Karbala, in Iraq, in 680. There, the followers of Hussein, numbering fewer than 200 including women and children, were cut down by an Umayad force of 4,000.

Hussein's severed head, it was reported, was taken to Damascus, the Umayad capital in Syria. There the Umayad caliph, Yazid I, struck it across the mouth with his cane. For Shia Muslims, this was the ultimate betrayal, for Hussein was Muhammad's grandson and the prophet himself had once kissed those lips.

Karbala, in Iraq, the scene of Hussein's defeat, now became the second of the holiest cities for Shia Muslims. At the same time, the great schism, or division, between Shia and Sunni Muslims became complete, with the Shia a minority and living mainly in southern Iraq.

Shia Islam did not take hold in neighboring Iran for many centuries. It was introduced by the dynasty known as the Safavids, who ruled from 1501 to 1722. With Shia Islam the state religion, the first Safavid leader, Ismail, proclaimed himself both a spiritual authority and a secular ruler. He and some of the early Safavids temporarily set an example for the Islamic Republic of Iran that was to come into existence nearly 500 years later. An invasion by Afghanistan that captured the Safavid city of Isfahan brought the dynasty to an end.

THE ATTEMPTED REFORMS OF THE PAHLAVI SHAHS OF IRAN

The years after the demise of the Safavids in 1732 saw Iran slip into a tribal society of petty kingdoms until unification and revival of the monarchy by a dynasty known as the Qajars in the late 1700s. The Qajar shahs, who remained in power until 1925, were for the most part despotic rulers. Although they represented themselves as the shadow of God on earth, they indulged in worldly pleasures and taxed the population heavily, leading to demands in the early 1900s for a constitution and a parliament to curb the absolutism of the monarchy.

The 1800s also saw the growth of interest by both Great Britain and Russia in Iran, with both nations seeking concessions to develop industrial projects in the building of railways, in mining, and in oil exploration, and seeking to grow markets for their commercial goods. By the time the first of the two Pahlavi shahs, Reza Khan, came on the scene in 1925, Iran had become involved in international affairs and was looking to the West for modernization and reform of the old order.

Reza Khan, now known as Reza Shah, adopted the family name Pahlavi, which actually was the name of Iran's pre-Islamic language. A former military officer, he built a strong army and developed the nation's industry and its consumer economy. Most notably, Reza Shah tried to control the Islamic elements in Iran that prevented secular, or nonreligious, education and restricted the rights of women.

Under the Qajars, girls could be married as young as the age of nine, in keeping with Islamic law. Though child marriage continued under Reza Shah, he raised the legal marriage age for women to eighteen. He also introduced a secular educational system that included schools for girls. In 1931, women were given the right to file for divorce, and in 1934 Reza Shah opened the University of Tehran as a coeducational school, an important step in making a university education available to women. At the same time, Reza Shah attempted to ban the wearing of the *chador*, the all-in-one hooded long garment that was required for women under Islamic law.

The chador, also often referred to as the veil because of the portion that was designed to cover a woman's hair exposing only the face, continued to be worn by older and more traditional women, however. Increasingly, Reza Shah's attempted reforms brought him into conflict with the nation's religious leaders. He had gone too far in trying to make social and educational changes. Also, as World War II began, Great Britain accused him of having pro-German sympathies, and on September 16, 1941, Reza Shah abdicated in favor of his son, who ascended the throne as Mohammed Reza Shah Pahlavi.

During the reign of the second Pahlavi Shah, lasting from 1941 to his exile early in 1979, the United States developed a closer relationship with Iran. The nation was seen as an important obstacle to the development of Communism in the Middle East, and to strengthen it against the Soviet threat, a string of United States presidents supplied the Shah with military and technical support, and a variety of beneficial trade agreements.

The Shah of Iran (who ruled from 1941–1979), shown here with his wife, tried to control the Islamic elements that prevented secular education and restricted women's rights.

However, with the election of Jimmy Carter to the United States presidency in 1976, a new approach to Iran was taken. Carter feared that the Shah's dictatorial powers, his indifference to the Iranian constitution and its parliament, his secret police force, and his luxurious and flamboyant lifestyle might lead to revolution and he urged the Shah to make reforms and pay more attention to human rights. Early in 1977, a high-ranking official of Carter's administration expressed the president's views with the following words. "This is a new administration. If the Shah thinks he will get anything he wants in the arms field, he is in for a big surprise."

Awed by the diplomatic setback, the Shah attempted to make some domestic reforms beginning in 1977. It was too late, however, to receive strong enough support from the United States or to hold out against the gathering storm at home that was being fomented by the Ayatollah Khomeini from abroad. By 1979, Mohammed Reza Shah Pahlavi and his regime were swept away by the overpowering force of an Islamic revolution.

THE ONSET OF THE ISLAMIC REVOLUTION IN IRAN

"I do not remember what I was doing or where I was on that Sunday when I first heard the news that the American embassy had been occupied by a ragtag group of students."

These are the words of foreign-educated Azar Nafisi, an Iranian woman and a professor of English literature who returned to Iran in the revolutionary year of 1979 to teach at the University of Tehran and who was expelled for refusing to wear the veil.

Nonetheless Nafisi remained in Iran until 1997, and in her book *Reading Lolita in Tehran,* published in 2003, she tells of her eighteen years of life in the Islamic Republic.

During the last two years of that time, Nafisi gathered former women students at her home to discuss forbidden works of Western literature.

Describing the appearance of the embassy on the days following the takeover, Nafisi tells us that they were covered with slogans that read: THIS IS NOT A STRUGGLE BETWEEN THE U.S. AND IRAN, IT'S A STRUGGLE BETWEEN ISLAM AND BLASPHEMY! THE MORE WE DIE, THE STRONGER WE WILL BECOME!

The American embassy was now known as the "nest of spies," and the revolutionary government of Ayatollah Khomeini broadened the hatred for the United States by transporting Iranians from all over the country to Tehran. "People were bused in daily," Nafisi writes,

> from the provinces and villages who didn't even know where America was, and sometimes thought they were actually being taken to America. They were given food and money, and they could stay and joke and picnic with their families in front of the nest of spies—in exchange, they were asked to demonstrate, to shout, "Death to America," and every now and then to burn the American flag.

Already, on April 1, 1979, Khomeini had proclaimed the establishment of the Islamic Republic of Iran, based on a ballot that excluded all political groups other than the one favoring a strict Islamic form of government. A constitution would be drafted that would establish a state dominated by the Shia clergy. In December 1979, the constitution was approved in a national referendum by over 98 percent of the vote, according to government figures.

Although there would be parliamentary elections, an elected president of the republic, vice-presidents, and cabinet posts, no person would be permitted to stand for election without the approval of the Ayatollah Khomeini and the religious hierarchy. Thus, any hopes for liberalization of the laws of Islam, known as *Sharia*, by elected officials would be nonexistent. Among Shia Muslims, Sharia, or Islamic canon law, includes the Koran, the sayings of the Prophet Muhammad, and those of the Twelve Imams.

Hatred for the Shah, who had fled the country on January 16, 1979, was so intense that in May the head of Iran's Revolutionary Court declared that the former ruler and his family were under a death sentence. Devout Muslims were encouraged to perform an assassination and were offered a free trip to Mecca for "carrying out the people's verdict."

Immediately following the embassy takeover in November, the United States broke ties with Iran, stopped a shipment of $300 million worth of military spare parts, cut off oil imports from Iran, and froze Iranian assets in the United States. Iranian diplomats and some Iranian students were expelled.

Although the Ayatollah released more than a dozen hostages, including women, African Americans, and non-Americans, in late November, those that remained were threatened with death, especially if the United States attempted a rescue mission. The return of the Shah to Iran for trial with his entire fortune was the only condition for the release of the hostages.

By April 1980, all efforts by the United Nations and other third parties to negotiate a release had failed, and President Jimmy Carter ordered a secret rescue mission. Helicopters bearing U. S. commando forces attempted a landing in the Iranian desert but encountered technical problems resulting in a crash and the deaths of eight service personnel.

Even after the Shah died in Egypt on July 27, 1980, Iran held out, setting conditions calling for the return of the Shah's wealth and the unlocking of Iran's frozen assets in the United States. It also continued to threaten to put the hostages on trial and possibly execute them.

November 4, 1980, saw two major events: the one-year anniversary of the hostage-taking and Jimmy Carter's defeat in the presidential election. Carter had largely been blamed for ineffectiveness in dealing with Iran. It was only on January 20, 1981, the inauguration day of the new president, Ronald Reagan, that Iran finally agreed to free the hostages after their ordeal of 444 days in captivity.

LIFE INSIDE THE ISLAMIC REPUBLIC OF IRAN

To understand how every aspect of life has been affected in Iran from the time of the Islamic revolution to the present, it is necessary to examine the far-reaching powers of the *faqih*. Faqih is the Islamic term for a supreme Shia religious leader, as represented by Iran's first faqih, Ayatollah Ruhollah Khomeini.

Through the faqih, all branches of government—executive, legislative, and judicial—are completely controlled, as are the military, the police, and the Revolutionary Guards in charge of enforcing social and moral behavior in the Islamic Republic.

Changes that were almost immediate, following the adoption of the Islamic constitution in December 1979, affected women, family life, marriage, Iran's educational system, and the rights of religious minorities. Freedom of expression in the press, on radio and television, in films, and in the arts was placed under severe scrutiny.

An Amnesty International Report

The waves of executions of Iran's "anti-revolutionaries" drew immediate protests from international human rights organizations. Ayatollah Khomeini's response was, "Criminals should not be tried. The trial of a criminal is against human rights. Human rights demand that we should have killed them in the first place when it became known that they were criminals." From the Amnesty International Newsletter, dated July 1982, volume XII, number 7, comes the following report concerning a young man executed in Tehran on January 31, 1982.

Name: Omid Gharib
Sex: male
Date of Arrest: 9 June 1980
Place of Arrest: Tehran
Place of Detention: Tehran, Qasr Prison
Charges: Being Westernized, brought up in a Westernized family; staying too long in Europe for his studies; smoking Winston cigarettes; displaying leftist tendencies.
Sentence: three years' imprisonment; death
Trial Information: The accused was tried behind closed doors. He was arrested after the authorities intercepted a letter he had sent to his friend in France. He was sentenced to three years' imprisonment in 1980. On February 2, 1982, while Omid Gharib was serving his prison term, his parents learned that he was executed. The circumstances surrounding his execution are not known.

Above all, the new powers of the *faqih* led to the persecution of Iranians who were suspected of being political enemies of the new regime.

Secularists, intellectuals, and liberals, as well as members of leftist, monarchist, and moderate Islamic parties were among those subject to arrest, violent treatment, forced public confessions, jail terms, and execution by firing squad. Common criminals were punished under Sharia law. A thief could have his hands or legs amputated. A woman accused of adultery or prostitution could be stoned to death.

Women, family life, and marriage were strongly affected by the Islamic revolution. Under the two Pahlavi shahs, whose rule had extended from 1925 to early 1979, efforts had been made to Westernize the role of women, through education and through opportunities to enter the work force on a variety of levels. In 1963 women had been given the right to vote and to hold public office. Women did not have to wear the veil in public and were, in fact, encouraged not to under the Pahlavi regimes.

Yet, it cannot be denied that under Mohammad Reza Shah Pahlavi, in spite of his modern views, there was a cultural, if not a religious bias, against women. In an interview with Italian journalist Oriana Fallaci, the Shah stated his belief that: "Women are important in a man's life only if they are beautiful and charming and keep their femininity. . . . You've never produced a Michelangelo or a Bach. . . . You've never produced a great chef."

An immediate effect of the Islamic revolution, however, was the clamping down on women's dress, demeanor, and behavior as never before. *Hejab*, or proper modest attire for women appearing in public, was strictly enforced. The headscarf and long robe or the all-in-one chador must show no hair or skin other than that of the face, which was to be free of makeup. Long or painted fingernails must be covered with black gloves.

In public, women were to behave modestly, not to talk loudly, sing, or do anything to draw attention to themselves. They were to be accompanied, when at all possible, by a father, brother, or husband, and were not to look directly at other men or to shake hands with members of the opposite sex. On entering a bus, a woman was to use the rear door and sit in the segregated section in the back.

Slogans appearing on the walls of buildings in the Islamic Republic, by order of Ayatollah Khomeini, read: VEILING IS A WOMAN'S PROTECTION. MY SISTER, GUARD YOUR VEIL. MY BROTHER, GUARD YOUR EYES.

For those women who were deemed to have dressed or behaved immodestly, there were the so-called morality police that patrolled the streets in white Toyota automobiles, with four officers, male and female, armed with guns. The cars were usually followed by minibuses, which took those who were apprehended off to jail. There they often received floggings and were put to work washing toilets. Some women were even subjected to virginity tests. Men, too, who appeared un-Islamic because they did not have beards or wore neckties (aping a custom of the United States), were subject to such arrests. Also, couples not related by blood or marriage who shared a table in a pastry shop or coffee shop were all too likely to be apprehended and removed by police units such as the Revolutionary Guards.

While the official marriage ages before the Islamic revolution were eighteen for women and twenty-one for men, lower-class and rural Iranians had always married at younger ages. With the return of Islamic law, girls could now officially be married as young as the age of nine. Islamic men were permitted to have as many as four wives. Also, in keeping with Shia law, there is a specially recognized form of temporary marriage, known as *muta*. No limit exists on the number of muta marriages a man may contract. Such marriages may last for hours or years depending on the circumstances. Traditionally, muta marriages were common during pilgrimages to holy shrines at some distance from home, on which wives did not accompany their husbands.

On the positive side, family life appears to have been strengthened with the imposition of the Islamic revolution. Traditionally the husband and father had been the head of the household in Iranian society, but the new restrictions on wives and daughters now give male relatives even greater authority.

As might be expected, young Iranian women with more secular views are likely to clash with male family members on issues of dress, travel, and freedom of movement. With summer temperatures in Tehran, for example, reaching the upper 90s, women during the recent summer of 2004 attempted to wear clothing that was lighter in both color and weight—an option that appeared to have been accepted by the authorities for some previous summers. With the return of a more conservative government in February 2004, however, came a crackdown that once again meant fines, imprisonment, and flogging for those whose dress was seen as a source of "social corruption." This was true especially among those Iranian women who today make up a majority of university students in Iran.

Other aspects of life inside the Islamic Republic of Iran that have been in effect from 1979 to the present have to do with the censorship of western influences in the media and with the status and treatment of religious minorities.

As soon as the revolution took hold, publishing houses and bookstores that produced or sold western literature were either closed or carefully scrutinized for output such as "immoral fiction." Movie theaters were prohibited from showing films from the west or elsewhere that were considered offensive to Islam and television programs were similarly monitored by the state.

In 1989, Iran's condemnation of literature that was offensive to Islam reached beyond the nation's borders. The writer Salman Rushdie, a Muslim born in Bombay, India, in 1947, and living in Great Britain, published his fourth novel, titled *The Satanic Verses.*

The book was an irreverent fantasy that dealt with the life of the Prophet Muhammad and the birth of Islam. Although it won a prestigious book award in Britain, *The Satanic Verses* raised violent protests in a number of countries with Muslim populations, such as India, Pakistan, and Egypt, and in Muslim communities in England and even in Berkeley, California, where stores carrying the book were firebombed.

The Ayatollah Khomeini's wrath went even further. On February 14, 1989, he issued a *fatwa*, or condemnation, carrying a penalty of death, on Rushdie, calling his book "blasphemous against Islam," and on February 24 placing a bounty of $3 million in United States currency on the author's head. Rushdie was subsequently forced to live in hiding under British-financed security.

Later that year, on June 3, 1989, Khomeini died, but the *fatwa* was not lifted and, although Rushdie continued to write and publish, he lived in secrecy until the late 1990s. Today there are still conflicting reports as to whether Islamic fundamentalists, sanctioned or not by the government of Iran, may yet intend to carry out the death sentence. Rushdie, however, has apparently

Women and University Education in Iran

In spite of the numerous restrictions placed on women in the Islamic Republic, they currently make up 65 percent of university entrants in the country. How has this come about and what does it portend for the future of this Islamic nation?

Soon after Mohammad Reza Shah Pahlavi went into exile in 1979, he conceded that one of his mistakes had been to encourage university attendance on a major scale during his regime. "I moved too rapidly in opening the doors of the universities, without imposing a more severe preliminary selection. The entrance exams were too easy," he stated.

Whether the Shah's assessment was correct or not, one of the first acts of the Islamic revolution was to close down all universities from 1979 to 1981. The purpose was to change the curricula to eliminate secular elements that were considered offensive to Islam, to purge faculty and students who were considered disloyal to the revolution, and to set new standards for examinations, as well as for student admissions and the hiring of faculty.

Changes were also made along these lines on the elementary and secondary levels in public education. Religious schools known as *madrasahs,* run by the Shia clergy for the education of the young, had long existed in Iran, and these expanded their registration markedly with the coming of the revolution.

When the universities finally did reopen later in the 1980s, all female students and faculty members were required to wear the veil and they were checked daily on entering the campus for improper garb, the wearing of makeup or jewelry, and the contents of their purses. Although these restrictions have for the most part remained in place to the present, a new generation of women seeking higher education has grown up in Iran, and the year 1998 saw more women than men taking university entrance exams.

Slowly, educated women have been finding employment outside the home and have been particularly active in campaigning for women's rights, especially pertaining to divorce, inheritance, and child custody laws. Progress has varied depending on the severity of the religious authorities, but there are hopeful signs that the second generation, known as the "children of the revolution," will make their voices heard for reform.

decided that it is relatively safe to make public appearances and has even allowed press coverage of his fourth marriage, in 2004, to an Indian actress/model.

While Shia Islam, the official religion of the theocratic nation of Iran, demands the highest degree of respect and obeisance, other religions have not fared so well since the establishment of the Islamic Republic. The fewest conflicts appear to be those between Iran's 90 percent of Shia Muslims and 8 percent of Sunni Muslims, in part because the Sunnis tend to live in the border regions of the country. While Shia and Sunni Muslims do share the five basic pillars of the faith, the Shia view the Sunni religion as incomplete. This is so because the Sunni do not accept the doctrine of the Twelfth Imam, as descended from the line of Ali, or the concept of the return of the Hidden Imam in the form of the Mahdi, or messiah.

Largest among the non-Muslim minorities in Iran are the Bahais. Bahaism originated in Iran in the 1840s as a reformist movement in Shia Islam. Bahais prospered under the secularizing Pahlavi shahs, holding government posts, succeeding in business and the professions, and opening their own schools. The religion also flourished through incorporating beliefs from other world religions that stressed brotherhood, pacifism, and equality of the sexes. Under the Islamic Republic, however, the Bahais are seen as heretics from Islam. As a result they have had their schools closed, their religious leaders arrested, their property rights attacked, and have become a persecuted minority barred from university attendance and many forms of work.

Most Christians in Iran are of Armenian or Assyrian origin and, while they are officially recognized as a religious minority under the 1979 constitution and are allowed to follow their own marriage and divorce laws, they are also required to follow Islamic customs. Christians must wear correct attire, women must wear the veil in public and in the schools, the sexes must be separated at public gatherings, and the use of alcohol is forbidden.

The Jewish community in Iran was, until the Islamic revolution, one of the oldest in the world. Its members were descended from the Jews who were liberated by the Persians from Babylonian captivity in 539 BCE and who chose to remain in the region. Under the Pahlavi shahs, Jews were concentrated in the larger cities and were active in business and the professions, and had great social and economic mobility.

Although the 1979 constitution recognized Jews as an official minority, Iran's intense hostility toward the State of Israel (which it sees as oppressing its Palestinian Muslims) made life uncomfortable for its Jewish population. Accusations of spying for Israel, resulting in arrests and even some executions of Jews, led to large-scale emigration after the fall of the Shah. Most of Iran's departing Jewish population, starting in the late 1970s and the early 1980s, subsequently settled in the United States.

THE POLITICAL LEADERSHIP OF IRAN SINCE KHOMEINI

The Ayatollah Ruhollah Khomeini, having suffered from heart problems since the early 1980s, died of a heart attack on June 3, 1989. The nation went into intense mourning for a period of five days, bringing enormous crowds to his gravesite. This outpouring of grief was followed by forty days of official mourning.

Khomeini's chosen successor was the Ayatollah Ali Khamenei, who had already served two successive four-year terms as president of Iran, from 1981 to 1989. As the Ayatollah Khamenei was of a slightly lower rank in the religious hierarchy of Iran than his predecessor, the constitution had to be amended to allow for his succession, which was based on the rigorously conservative views that he held.

As the current Supreme Leader of Iran, Khamenei has maintained many of the same policies as Khomeini, especially his denunciation of the United States and his refusal to give in to what he considered pro-reform or dissident movements within the country. In 1997, Khamenei clashed with a higher-ranking ayatollah, who questioned Khamenei's powers, remanding the ayatollah to house arrest. In 2003, Khamenei clamped down on pro-reform students who rioted, and he has been notorious for closing down newspapers that have published so-called anti-Islamic articles, and of sending their editors and staff members to jail.

In spite of the reactionary position taken by Supreme Leader Ayatollah Khamenei following his 1989 accession to Iran's highest spiritual and governmental post, there was a brief period of hope for liberalization with the election in 1997 of a new president of the Islamic Republic, Mohammad Khatami.

The Iran-Iraq War

Before closing the chapter on the legacy of the Ayatollah Ruhollah Khomeini, it is necessary to examine the war between Iran and the neighboring country of Iraq that broke out on September 22, 1980, and that lasted until August 1988. It is estimated that the Iran-Iraq War took close to a million lives, wounded one to two million, and involved about 40 percent of the male population of both countries. It ended after eight years in a cease-fire that the Ayatollah Khomeini referred to as "drinking the cup of poison."

The roots of the conflict ran deep. Iraq was led by the harshly dictatorial President Saddam Hussein, who favored his nation's Sunni minority over its Shia majority, and who felt threatened by the rise of Shia power in Iran following the 1979 revolution. Iraq, at that time, had the support of the United States, and when Saddam Hussein sent his Iraqi army over the Iranian border, Khomeini responded with a counterattack. He sought affirmation for his new revolutionary government and a victory that would strengthen Iran against both Iraq and the United States.

Many other elements, such as disputes about borders, navigation rights, and oil shipments underlay the hostility between the two nations. Foremost, however, were the religious and cultural Iraq-Iran antipathies, including those of Sunni versus Shia, Arabs versus Persians, and a secular government in Iraq versus a militant Islamic one in Iran.

As the war proceeded along the 730-mile border between Iran and Iraq, each nation took its turn on the offensive. Iran suffered air and missile attacks on its civilian population in Tehran and on its oilfields. The main toll of the war for Iran, however, included the deaths of boys as young as twelve and thirteen recruited into its "Army of Twenty Million" to clear minefields on the front lines.

Khatami had served in the revolutionary government as minister of culture and Islamic guidance from 1982 to 1992. He was, however, considered so much of a moderate with regard to the censorship of publications, films, and art that he was eventually forced to resign because of too much permissiveness.

His being allowed to stand for election as president in 1997 was a pleasant surprise for pro-reformists and he was strongly supported by moderates, intellectuals, students, women, and especially the younger generation that had grown up in the years following the 1979 revolution. However, the all-powerful Ayatollah Khamenei and other religious hard-line conservatives strongly opposed Khatami's political,

Shirin Ebadi, winner of the 2003 Nobel Peace Prize, is a rare example of an Iranian woman who practices law and has become a fearless advocate for women's rights. Inset is a photo of Ebadi and two other Nobel Peace Prize laureates.

Shirin Ebadi and the Struggle for a Reformed Islam

Unlike Judaism and Christianity, Islam has long been considered a religion that has resisted reform. Shirin Ebadi, however, is in the forefront of those who would bring tolerance and social equality into Islam, as it is practiced today in Iran and elsewhere.

Shirin Ebadi's biography written by the Norwegian Nobel Committee describes the lawyer and human rights activist as follows:

> Ebadi represents Reformed Islam, and argues for a new interpretation of Islamic law which is in harmony with vital human rights such as democracy, equality before the law, religious freedom, and freedom of speech. As for religious freedom, it should be noted that Ebadi also includes the rights of members of the Bahai community, which has had problems in Iran ever since its [1979 Islamic Republic] foundation.

social, and cultural reform efforts, and the new president was able to make little progress toward liberalization. Although Khatami was reelected for a second four-year term with more than three-fourths of the vote in 2001, it had become evident that little could be expected in the way of social and political progress before his presidency ended in 2005.

It was during the eight-year period (1997–2005) of Khatami's presidency, however, that some hopeful signs of democratization did begin to appear. Among them were the advancement of women and greater freedom of expression by the press.

An outstanding example of an Iranian woman who fought the conservative judiciary to obtain women's rights in matters of divorce and inheritance is the fifty-six-year-old lawyer and activist Shirin Ebadi who, in 2003, became the first Muslim and the first Iranian woman to win the Nobel Peace Prize.

Ebadi's path has been difficult. In 1975, prior to the Islamic revolution, this graduate of Tehran University was the first female judge in Iran, serving as president of the Tehran city court. With the onset of the Islamic revolution in 1979, Ebadi was forced to resign her post because women were not considered adequate to serve as judges.

Nonetheless, Ebadi established a law practice in the Islamic Republic, taking on political criminal cases, including the serial murders by stabbing of a number of students and liberal intellectuals in 1998 and 1999. She was deeply involved in the promotion of human rights, including those of women and children. In spite of having been imprisoned a number of times, she lectured at Tehran University during Khatami's presidency.

Hope for the future of the Islamic Republic of Iran during the Khatami years also rested, although often tenuously, in the area of reform journalism. While more than one hundred newspapers were shut down for political criticism of the government in the year 2000 alone, young journalists were able to find new ways to get the attention of the public. They accomplished this by putting their emphasis on social and cultural issues on the national scene, rather than directly on political matters.

It is impossible, for example, to criticize the Supreme Leader Ayatollah Khamenei, the judiciary (which has the power to shut down newspapers), or the members of the clergy (who are the pillars of the republic). However, it has not been directly forbidden to write about and graphically illustrate disturbing news items such as the high rate of traffic accidents in Iran, the country's poor rescue and fire services, the tragic human consequences of the Iran-Iraq War, or the salaries and working conditions of government employees.

One reformist newspaper forced to offer an apology to the government, after having been shut down for fifteen days, began trying this new approach in the year 2003 with what appeared to be success. The name of the newspaper was *Shargh*, meaning East, and it was staffed by "children of the Revolution" with an average age of twenty-five, many of whom have already served jail sentences as a result of having worked on newspapers that were shut down.

In 2004, *Shargh*, which was backed by private investors, had reached a circulation of 100,000. Whether, however, it would manage to stay on the newsstands depended largely on the outcome of the election of a new president for Iran to take place in June 2005. Already, conservative newspapers in Iran had charged *Shargh* with "working for America." When interviewed in late 2004, twenty-eight-year-old editor-in-chief Mohammad Ghoochani said, "The future of this country is my future. Some of it I can change; some of it I can't. But because we don't have a lot of choice we must be hopeful. We have no other choice but hope."

THE JUNE 2005 ELECTION OF IRANIAN PRESIDENT MAHMOUD AHMADINEJAD

During the closing years of the weakened Khatami presidency, the Ayatollah Khamenei and his clergy and judiciary jailed more and more student activists, shut down more newspapers and magazines, and vetoed an increasing number of legislative bills endorsed by the essentially powerless president. Nevertheless, hopes ran high among Iran's reformists for a new president who was at least a moderate and who would somehow be able to stand up to the ruling clergy with the support of the voters.

More than 1,000 would-be candidates attempted to enter the race. Of that number, only seven were approved by Supreme Leader Khamenei to stand for election. After the first balloting, the race tightened and a run-off election was held between the two principal winners. The result was a marked victory for the hard line, conservative mayor of Tehran—Mahmoud Ahmadinejad.

How had this nonreformer attained victory? The answer appeared to lie in his promises to Iran's poor and more traditional voters that

Mahmoud Ahmadinejad, elected president of Iran in 2005, is a hard-line leader who asserts Iran's rights to develop a nuclear power program.

he would end corruption and mismanagement and improve their economic status. Expanded health insurance, low-interest loans, lower prices, job creation, pay raises, and pensions appealed strongly to those people in the provinces who did not feel as politically oppressed as their more liberal and Western-looking compatriots in the cities.

Almost at once, Ahmadinejad's impact on the international scene was even stronger than within Iran. Threats during the Khatami presidency concerning enriching uranium for so-called peaceful energy purposes (but not excluding its use for nuclear weaponry) accelerated sharply after the new president took power. In the year following his election, Ahmadinejad undertook an alarming program of nuclear power development, declaring to European nations and the United States, "A nuclear program is our irrefutable right."

Western efforts to deal with Ahmadinejad during 2006 regarding his violation of the Nuclear Nonproliferation Treaty of the United Nations Security Council, through either threats or incentives, appeared unsuccessful. The road ahead also remained troubling. Iran has been a sponsor of international terrorism through its support of such groups operating against Israel as Hezbollah, Islamic Jihad, and Hamas. Ahmadinejad has declared that Israel should be wiped off the face of the earth and that the Holocaust was a myth. He also has the power to inflame the civil-war-like situation in Iraq by supporting Iran's coreligionist Shia majority over the Sunni minority. And, lastly, he controls a nation with a large oil supply that could easily become a global economic weapon. What does all this tell us about the world's singular Islamic theocracy?

The Ancient World: AN EGYPTIAN THEOCRACY   2 ■ ■

THEOCRACIES—GOVERNMENTS RULED BY GODLIKE KINGS or high-ranking religious leaders—have existed on earth since ancient times. Modern Iran, with its ayatollahs in control of every aspect of the nation's political, social, moral, cultural, and religious life, is only the most recent example of a theocratic society.

It is believed that the first use of the word theocracy appeared in the writings of Josephus, the Jewish historian and soldier who lived in the first century CE, from the year 37 to 100. Josephus was born in Jerusalem and served as a general between 66 and 73 in the Jewish struggle against the Roman conquest of ancient Israel.

When the Romans overcame his forces, Josephus chose surrender rather than suicide. Subsequently, he went to live in Rome and wrote a firsthand account of the fall of Jerusalem and the destruction of the Second Temple (the holy site and the center of Jewish religious belief and worship).

Under the patronage of the Roman imperial court, Josephus went on to write an entire history of the Jews from earliest times, as well as other works of religion, and his autobiography.

We learn from Josephus and from other sources relating to the Hebrew Bible (or Old Testament, much of it written in approximately 600 BCE) that the origins of Judaism probably date back to the year 1800 BCE. This was the time of Abraham, the first of the Jewish

Was the Earthly Kingdom of Ancient Israel a Theocracy?

The wandering tribes of ancient Israel did not unite into an earthly kingdom until about 1030 BCE under the first of the three so-called great kings, Saul, who was anointed by the Jewish priesthood to fight the surrounding enemy tribes and consolidate the holdings of the Jews. Saul was a war chief, rather than a divinely endowed ruler, and his mission was completed by King David, who married Saul's daughter, set up his capital in Jerusalem, and expanded the kingdom into an empire, all approximately during the years 1000 to 965 BCE.

The third of the great kings, Solomon, was the son of David. While it was he who built the great holy and single worship site of the Jews, the First Temple in Jerusalem, David, like his predecessors, was not considered a divinely endowed figure. All three of the great kings were essentially warriors and practical men, ambitious mainly for wealth and worldly power. So lavish, in fact, was the spending of Solomon that by 922 BCE excessive taxation brought down his empire and it split into two separate kingdoms that would eventually fall to powerful peoples from Mesopotamia (present-day Iraq), the Assyrians and the Babylonians.

The Babylonians destroyed the First Temple in 586 BCE and took many of the Jews back to their own land as captives. The priesthood that had served in Solomon's temple was disbanded and, as the years of captivity continued, it fell to the Hebrew prophets to carry the message of God to the scattered Jews of the former kingdoms. The Jews responded by setting up, wherever they were, their own small houses of worship known as synagogues.

So, we cannot strictly say that the Jews of the ancient kingly past lived in an earthly theocracy. Their rulers appear to have been servants of the lord rather than gods or god-endowed humans. As time passed, the ongoing fate of the Jews was to be forced to scatter even more widely across the face of the earth. However, the power that consolidated and maintained them as a people of a singular belief would continue to come directly from the God with which they had made their covenant in earliest times.

patriarchs, or fathers of the tribe, who was promised by God that he would become the father of a great people in return for his belief in a single and supreme deity.

Following God's instructions, Abraham led his clan from the city of Ur (in present-day Iraq) into the land we know as present-day Israel. Thus a new religion was born, one that cast aside the worship of images of so-called false gods and that made a solemn contract, or a covenant, with the one God to whom all believers were bound.

In his relationship with the Jewish people, the God of the Hebrew Bible can be said to be a theocratic ruler. In the Book of Genesis, Abraham is asked by God to sacrifice his son Isaac, and Abraham shows his loyalty and obedience to God through his willingness to perform this terrible deed. Before he can do so, however, God, having tested Abraham, relents and stays his hand, sparing the life of Isaac.

Later, in the Hebrew Bible's account of Moses, the lawgiver, God sends his people a set of rules that they are instructed to live by, known as the Ten Commandments. Moses, who according to the Bible led the Israelites out of slavery in Egypt, may be presumed to have lived in the 1300s BCE, or even as early as the 1500s.

The commandments were said to be inscribed on two stone tablets and to have been brought down by Moses from the top of Mount Sinai, believed to have been located on the triangular-shaped Sinai Peninsula, today the border between Egypt and Israel. They command the Jews to have no other God, to make no images of God, not to take the Lord's name in vain, and to remember the Jewish Sabbath and keep it holy. The Jews are instructed to honor their father and mother, not to kill, commit adultery, or steal, and lastly not to bear false witness against their neighbor or to desire or envy that which belongs to their neighbor.

The God of the Hebrew Bible appears, in every sense, to be a theocratic ruler. Every Jewish male infant must be circumcised as part of the covenant. The dietary laws known as *Kashrut* (purity), having to do with the separation of meat and dairy products, and banning the eating of pork and shellfish, must be observed. Shrines to other divinities must be destroyed. God's kingdom does not allow for deviations, and democracy, as understood to allow for the admission of nonbelievers, cannot flourish.

THE THEOCRATIC GOVERNMENT OF THE ANCIENT EGYPTIANS

Unlike Ancient Israel, with its shattered early empire, its broken and weakened kingdoms, and its succession of conquests of the Jewish people from outside the region, Ancient Egypt enjoyed a sustained history as a nation and an empire that lasted for the better part of 3,000 years. There is also a marked difference in the way the term theocracy can be applied to civilizations as unalike as those two—that of the ancient Jews and that of the ancient Egyptians.

When Josephus, writing in the first century CE used the term theocracy, he was referring to a people—the Jews—who had lived directly under the power and authority of God, rather than under the rulership of a divine or godlike earthly monarch.

In ancient Egypt, the situation with regard to religion and government was quite the opposite. There was not one god but many, and the supreme ruler of the land, who came to be known as the pharaoh, was regarded as a god. He or she was the earthly representative of divine power and, after death, enjoyed an afterlife of continuing intercession with the gods on behalf of his or her subjects.

As a result, deceased Egyptian monarchs were mummified to resemble as closely as possible the beings they had been in life, and were given sumptuous royal burials in tombs equipped with every necessity, convenience, and pleasure for the afterlife. The divine rulers of Egypt were also said to have joined or, in fact, become the god Osiris after death. For Osiris, the Egyptian god of the dead, was one of the most powerful deities in the pantheon.

How did the vast array of the ancient Egyptian gods develop and what was their impact on the rulership and on the lives of the governed?

As early as 5000 BCE, agriculture had begun to flourish on the banks of the Egyptian portion of the Nile, the world's longest river, which flows northward over 4,000 miles (6,400 kilometers) from Central Africa into the Mediterranean Sea. Although Egypt is mainly desert, it benefits yearly from the flooding of the lands along the river, which brings deposits of fertile silt as well as moisture to what would otherwise be a sandy wasteland.

As a result, early farming societies grew up along the watered "black lands" (as opposed to the "red lands," or deserts that lay beyond the

The Legend of Osiris and the Resurrection Myth

The story of Osiris, the Egyptian god of the dead, is one of making whole and functional again that which has been destroyed. According to legend, Osiris was himself once a much-beloved king who was murdered by his jealous brother, Set, through trickery.

After urging Osiris to climb into a lidded box, Set sealed the lid and cast the box into the Nile River. The box floated out to sea but was rescued by Isis, the wife of Osiris, who brought his body back to Egypt. Set then stole the corpse of Osiris and cut it into fourteen parts, scattering them all over Egypt. Again, Isis worked her magic, collecting the fragments and restoring Osiris's dismembered body back to wholeness and life.

As a result, one purpose of the Egyptian funeral rites was to identify the deceased monarch with the god Osiris so that he would rise from the dead and rule in heaven with him. Well-preserved paintings on the ancient tomb walls of Egypt often show the royal occupant dressed as Osiris, wearing the crown and the false beard of the living monarch but wrapped in the linen bandages of the mummified dead.

river's reach). It was discovered that domesticated strains of wheat and barley could be grown for basic sustenance, followed, as time passed, by many kinds of vegetables and of fruits such as grapes, dates, and pomegranates. It was no wonder that Herodotus, the Greek historian who visited Egypt centuries later in the 400s BCE, named it "the gift of the Nile." He remarked that farmers had to do little more than scatter their seed in the moist soil and allow cattle to trample it into the ground in order to produce a bountiful harvest.

It soon became evident to the early Nile dwellers that there were a number of natural forces that affected their lives. These included the annual flooding of the Nile, the rising and setting of the sun that helped the crops to grow, the phases of the moon, as well as the movements of the stars, which predicted the Nile inundation. As a result, they began to create an array of gods ascribed to natural phenomena that became the basis of their religion.

Principal among the nature gods was Ra (or Re), the god of the sun, who would be represented in stone carvings and on painted tomb walls as having a human body with the head of a falcon, crowned by a disk that symbolized the sun. A god called Hapi, sometimes shown as a pair of gods, personified the Nile. His fleshy, thickset body represented the abundance that its silted waters produced and he often wore a headdress of the plants that grew in the Nile shallows, such as water lilies and papyrus (the source of the Egyptians' writing paper).

Isis, the wife of Osiris, was, among other things, the goddess of nature, and there was even an earth god called Geb and a sky goddess named Nut. Later, as farming became more advanced and Egypt grew from a string of farming villages and small city-states into a nation with a unified government, there was leisure time for the pursuit of crafts, writing, music, dancing, and other activities beyond the raising of crops. Gods were assigned to these aspects of human creativity, as well as to the all-important process of mummification.

The unification of Egypt under a single ruler took place in about 3100 BCE, when a king known as Narmer, and sometimes as Menes, expanded his holdings in the southern part of the country to take over the northern portion as well. Henceforth, the Egyptian kings would wear the so-called double crown, a combination of the pear-shaped white crown of the south and the boxy red crown of the north.

From the start, the unified government of Egypt was a sacred monarchy, in which the divine nature of the ruler was never questioned. It was based on his godliness as well as his relationship to the other gods, and his position was supported, as Egypt grew and prospered, by a vast priesthood that attended the chief gods in their great stone temples. Principal among these gods, during the period of expansion and wealth known as the New Kingdom (1550 to 1070 BCE), was the god Amun (also called Amen, Amon), who was highly regarded by the Egyptian rulers as having brought them success.

The powerful priests of Egypt were known as the servants of the gods. In the great pillared temple of Karnak, which can be visited today in the Egyptian city of Luxor, priests with shaved heads and dressed in fine white linen attended the stone statue of the god in its inner sanctuary. It was their duty to wake him in the morning, offer food and drink, and burn incense in his honor. So holy was the image that the Egyptian people, who had no access to the temple, saw the statue only on festival days, perhaps once or twice a year.

In spite of the formalities that separated the kings, priests, and other high-ranking members of the religious hierarchy from the farmers, laborers, weavers, craftspeople, and others of lower rank, the Egyptian ruler had a number of responsibilities toward the governed. One of the principal goddesses of Egypt in its most developed period was Maat, the goddess of peace, truth, and justice. Order, balance, and harmony in the workings of society were among the demands of Maat, as opposed to chaos, which was seen as a threat to the very existence of the Egyptian nation.

Not all of Egypt's rulers were as accountable to the governed as they might have been, and there were so-called Intermediate Periods during Egypt's long history when there were governmental breakdowns and incursions by foreigners. So highly valued, however, was the principle of justice that one of the main features of the funeral ceremony of the mummified royalty of Egypt was the symbolic weighing of the heart on a balance scale against the weight of a feather. It was believed that if the heart were found to be heavier than a feather, the deceased would not be permitted to enter the afterlife.

THE GROWTH OF SCIENCE AND THE ARTS IN THE EGYPTIAN THEOCRACY

The ancient Egyptians were to prove themselves masters of mathematics, the calendar, and the movements of the heavens, of writing, of architecture and building, of sculpture, painting, crafts, and jewelry.

Once farming communities had been established along the Nile and organized into nomes, or provinces, under an increasingly unified government, there began to be leisure time for activities beyond the production of food, clothing, and shelter. Another factor accounting for the many accomplishments of the ancient Egyptians was their geographic isolation, guaranteeing freedom from invasion throughout much of their long history.

The valley of the life-giving Nile was bordered on the east and on the west by forbidding deserts. Infiltration from the portion of Africa that lay to the south of Egypt was hampered by the cataracts of the Nile, rocky terrain through which the river's rapids cascaded before it entered Egypt proper. Major inroads, when they did come, approached Egypt from Asia via the Mediterranean Sea.

Most important for the cultivation of the sciences and the arts was the theocratic rulership of Egypt. Early on, local officials, as agents of the royal government, realized that records had to be kept detailing the height of the annual Nile flood and the sizes and boundaries of the farmers' fields. Also, to ensure good harvests, plans had to be drawn up for irrigation systems and other public works. Lastly, there had to be a means of determining the amount of taxes the farmers were to pay on the harvested crops.

This demand for educated people who could read, write, and do mathematical calculations resulted in the development of the important and honorable occupation of scribe. Even the young sons of farmers could be admitted to the scribal schools, starting at the age of six or seven, to study the complicated hieroglyphics that were the basis of the ancient Egyptian written language. Scribes also engaged in the writing of government laws and proclamations, in funeral texts such as the Book of the Dead (to guide the deceased through the afterlife), and in the writing of poetry, songs, and stories.

All government officials were required to be literate. Scribes, therefore, had the opportunity to rise to high office. The highest such rank was the king's vizier, his closest advisor. Priests, too, were highly educated, and many were healers and even lawyers and judges. Thoth was the Egyptian god of writing. He was depicted as having the body of a human and the head of an ibis, a long-billed, long-legged wading

The Pyramids of Khufu, Khafre, and Menkaure

The so-called Great Pyramid of Egypt rises to a height of 450 feet (135 meters) and is composed of more than 2 million blocks of stone, each weighing about 2.5 tons. Inside this monument, the Fourth Dynasty ruler Khufu (also known by his Greek name, Cheops) was entombed in a royal chamber accessed by ramps within the pyramid.

Two smaller, but also large and imposing, pyramids that rise nearby were built as magnificent memorials to house the bodies of two of Khufu's successors, the kings known as Khafre and Menkaure. As both Khufu's mummified body and his rich tomb furnishings were later stolen from his burial chamber, the tombs of Khufu's successors were designed to lie beneath rather than within their pyramids. The underground chambers could only be approached via shafts with secret openings that lay at some distance from the pyramids themselves. But these tombs, too, were discovered and robbed.

The Greek traveler and historian Herodotus was told that it had taken twenty years and the labor of 100,000 men to build the Great Pyramid of Khufu. Contrary to popular belief at one time, the builders of the pyramids were not slaves or foreign captives. They were for the most part Egyptian farmers, who, during the months when the Nile was flooding its banks, were neither planting, growing, nor harvesting their crops. The construction crews labored willingly on the monuments

The three great pyramids at Giza, as seen from the Nile, attest to the wealth and power of the theocratic rulers of the Old Kingdom.

because their religion assured them that the proper entombment of their godlike rulers meant that there would be peace and prosperity for all their subjects throughout eternity.

In turn, the government provided food, clothing, living quarters, and other necessities for the crews who worked on the pyramid sites. In addition to the laborers who quarried, trimmed, and raised the huge blocks of stone, toolmakers, artisans, overseers, scribes, and government officials were part and parcel of the great building projects.

Nor did the three great pyramids stand in isolation. They were surrounded by numerous other structures. These included smaller pyramids for other members of the royal family, as well as flat-roofed rectangular graves known as *mastabas*, and temples to the gods as well as mortuary temples for the royal departed.

bird of the Nile. Often he carried a scroll of papyrus in one hand and a quill in the other.

For the development of architecture, beginning with the great pyramids of Egypt, history is indebted to the obsession of its rulers with building grandiose monuments in which to spend eternity. The unification of Egypt in 3100 BCE led from an early dynastic period (covering Dynasties 0 to 2) to a flowering of wealth and power known as the Old Kingdom (Dynasties 3 to 6) from 2649 to 2150 BCE. It was during the Fourth Dynasty that the three world-renowned pyramids at Giza, near present-day Cairo, were constructed.

The wealth of the kings of the Fourth Dynasty was due in part to the prosperity of the Egyptian economy. It was also the result of successful trading expeditions to the surrounding regions of Africa and the Middle East. From the southern reaches of the Nile and from the coast of present-day Somalia, the Egyptians imported such luxuries as ivory, gold, animal skins, and incense. The Sinai Peninsula offered turquoise and copper, while present-day Lebanon was a source of cedar logs for building wood, which Egypt lacked.

These imports, combined with native Egyptian products including stone, pottery, and leather, as well as a variety of minerals, resulted in the creation of magnificent works of art. They included statues and other kinds of sculpture for tombs and temples, richly painted surfaces, and exquisite crafts and jewelry to adorn the bodies of the deceased kings.

The age of the pyramids came to an end, however, with the passing of the Old Kingdom in about 2150 BCE. It was followed by a period of confusion known as the First Intermediate Period and then by another great age known as the Middle Kingdom (2030–1640 BCE) which was threatened by the invasions of an Asiatic people known as the Hyksos. Following a Second Intermediate Period, ancient Egypt reached its most expansive age with the onset of the New Kingdom (1550–1070 BCE). It was during this era that a short-lived effort was made by an Egyptian pharaoh to turn the nation away from its worship of many gods to that of a single god.

THE LEGACY OF THE EGYPTIAN THEOCRATIC STATE

The wealth and glory of the New Kingdom manifested itself in a number of ways. The survival of the body after death in mummified form remained a strong preoccupation of the royal families, for only with the body's preservation could an afterlife for the deceased be guaranteed.

The building of the pyramids of the Old Kingdom, however, such as the great monuments of the Fourth Dynasty, had long passed. The kings, queens, and nobles of the New Kingdom were buried in sumptuous tombs hewn out of natural rock in the cliffs that rose on the western side of the Nile at Thebes, today identified as the modern city of Luxor.

The tombs themselves consisted of a series of rooms including a magnificent burial chamber. Their walls were sculpted in relief or brilliantly painted with scenes from Egyptian life. They depicted everyday activities such as farming, fishing, and hunting, as well as banquets, entertainments, music and dancing, scenes of war, and religious events. The latter included details of mummification and funeral processions.

Similarly, the tombs were equipped with luxurious furnishings, items of clothing and personal use, such as perfumes and cosmetics, objects of gold, ivory, and ebony, and intricate jewelry. For all of these riches and valuable keys to the past, we are indebted to the religious beliefs of the theocratic rulers of ancient Egypt.

As time passed, and especially during the prosperous era of the New Kingdom, people of lesser rank also began to build tombs for themselves in the hope of taking part in an afterlife, and members of the general population practiced mummification.

Although social divisions existed in ancient Egypt, each class of society appeared to have operated in harmony with the other, and there were opportunities to move from farmer's son to scribe or from healer to priest. Especially reassuring was the regard for marriage, family life, and children, the respect for education, and the position of women.

Egyptian women were permitted to inherit and own property and, upon marriage, continued to control any assets they had brought to the union. They were allowed to bear witness in court, and there is even some evidence that they served as judges at one time.

In addition to managing the affairs of their households, the wives of the farming classes as well as others were permitted to work outside the home, performing such duties as servants, weavers of cloth, musicians, priestesses, and hired mourners at funerals.

Notable among Egypt's great rulers was the Eighteenth Dynasty queen Hatshepsut, who ruled for approximately twenty years from

A Theocratic Ruler as Religious Reformer

The New Kingdom was notable for the power and successes of the Eighteenth Dynasty, which flourished within it for generations. During its rule, the invading Hyksos were driven out of Egypt and back to Asia, which was then militarily invaded by the great pharaoh Thutmose III. Of all the gods in the Egyptian pantheon, the one who was most highly worshipped and heavily supported by the influential priesthood was the god Amun. For it was Amun who was mainly considered to have aided the Egyptians in the expansion of their empire.

In about 1349 BCE, however, along came a pharaoh who objected to the domination of the priests of Amun, as well as to the numerous other gods that his people worshiped. He chose to discard all of the existing gods and to elect for Egypt a single god, the Aten, or the disk of the sun. In doing so, he changed his official name of Amenhotep IV to the name Akhenaten ("pleasing to Aten").

Akhenaten perceived the sun as a symbol of the spirit of creation, upon which all living things depended, and he refused to think of such a god as taking human form. As part of his approach to monotheism, Akhenaten moved his capital northward from the traditional royal seat at Thebes to a new city located on the Nile that he called Akhetaten ("horizon of the Aten").

Akhenaten's reign, however, was brief. In the thirteen or so years during which he attempted to introduce the worship of a single god to Egypt, he neglected military affairs and the empire lost prestige abroad. Above all, the power of the priesthood and the conservative public, deeply attached to its numerous gods, proved too strong for Akhenaten's new form of spiritualism.

On Akhenaten's death, the nine-year-old pharaoh Tutankhamen (possibly a son, brother, or son-in-law of Akhenaten) came to the throne. The young king, who would become famous mainly because of the discovery of his magnificently appointed intact tomb in 1922, returned his capital to Thebes, where the reigning cult of the chief god Amun presided, and Egypt once again reverted to the worship of its numerous gods.

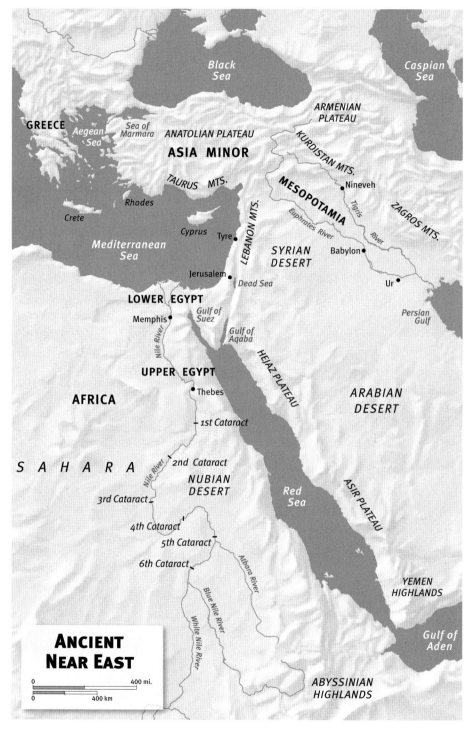

Black
Sea

Caspian
Sea

ARMENIAN
PLATEAU

GREECE Aegean Sea of
        Sea   Marmara ANATOLIAN PLATEAU

KURDISTAN MTS.

ASIA MINOR

TAURUS MTS.

MESOPOTAMIA

Nineveh

Tigris

ZAGROS MTS.

Rhodes

Crete

Euphrates River

River

Cyprus Tyre

LEBANON MTS.

Mediterranean
Sea

SYRIAN
DESERT

Babylon

Jerusalem

Dead Sea

Ur

LOWER EGYPT

Memphis

Gulf of
Suez

Persian
Gulf

Nile River

Gulf of
Aqaba

UPPER EGYPT

HEJAZ PLATEAU

ARABIAN
DESERT

AFRICA

Thebes

1st Cataract

S A H A R A

Nile River

2nd Cataract

NUBIAN
DESERT

ASIR PLATEAU

3rd Cataract

4th Cataract

Red
Sea

5th Cataract

6th Cataract

Atbara River

YEMEN
HIGHLANDS

Blue Nile River

**ANCIENT
NEAR EAST**

White Nile River

Gulf of
Aden

0   400 mi.

ABYSSINIAN
HIGHLANDS

0   400 km

The Ancient Near East

1479 to 1458 BCE. Often she was portrayed wearing the false beard and the royal crown of the great male pharaohs. Other sculptures show her as the beautiful woman that she was.

Daughter, wife, half-sister, stepmother, and aunt of three great pharaohs bearing the name of Thutmose, Hatshepsut distinguished herself through trading expeditions to what was known as the land of Punt, probably Somalia in the horn of Africa. A famous structure that Hatshepsut built is her pillared mortuary temple on the western side of the Nile in the cliffs near Thebes. Carved into the temple walls are scenes of the expeditions that Hatshepsut fostered, mainly in a peaceful fashion and for the purpose of enriching Egypt and further developing its trade and industry.

The theocratic nature of Egyptian rule continued through the Nineteenth Dynasty, and especially under its grandiose pharaoh Ramses II, who reigned for close to sixty-seven years, from 1279 to 1213 BCE. In addition to building enormous monuments to himself that were essentially personal portraits in stone, Ramses II attempted to extend and stabilize the Egyptian empire by invading the land of the Hittites, a powerful people based in present-day Turkey. His efforts to dominate them, however, led to a long war ending in a peace treaty that gave Ramses less than he had hoped for despite his claims of victory.

The death of Ramses II at the age of ninety or so marked the beginning of the end for the powerful Egyptian pharaohs, who were looked upon as divine figures. Among the dynasties that followed from about 1070 BCE on, there were rulers from beyond Egypt's borders, including Libyans from the west, Nubians from the south, and Syrians from Asia. The thirtieth and final of the Egyptian dynasties came to an end in 343 BCE. Conquests of Egypt by Persians, by the Macedonian Greek conqueror, Alexander the Great, and by Romans followed.

The old religion, however, with its emphasis on mummifying the dead to ensure the existence of an afterlife, was maintained even under rulers of foreign birth, or was melded with the customs of the newcomers. The Greeks, for example, who ruled Egypt for three hundred years (from 332 BCE under Alexander and ending with Cleopatra VII in 30 BCE) had followed the custom in their own land of burning the dead. But as rulers of Egypt, they adopted the process of mummification.

Similarly the Romans, who took command of Egypt after the death of Cleopatra, also turned to the making of mummies, often burying them in underground galleries known as catacombs. This practice was particularly true of families of wealth and prominence.

Finally, in 640 CE, the religion of Islam, which had been founded on the Arabian Peninsula only a short time earlier by the Prophet Muhammad, swept Egypt. The ancient Egyptian theocracy with its powerful divine rulers, its numerous gods, and its fervent belief in the power of the royal afterlife to protect the land and its people through eternity, was gone forever.

3
Mesoamerican Theocracies: ■ ■ ■
THE MAYA AND THE AZTECS

AS WE HAVE SEEN IN LOOKING at both contemporary Iran and ancient Egypt, the principal purpose of a theocratic form of government is to put religious laws into effect and to make certain that they are carried out.

In some cases, as in Islamic fundamentalist Iran, the 1979 revolution and the adoption of a constitution based on Sharia, or strict Islamic law, had wide-ranging effects on a society that had previously been freer and more open despite the rulership of a series of kings, or shahs. Almost every aspect of life and every member of society experienced some form of oppression under the all-embracing powers of the new religious leader, Ayatollah Khomeini.

The political, social, economic, cultural, and personal downsides of the new system of government appeared, to the outside world, to outweigh any positive accomplishments issuing from the change. As the Islamic revolution in Iran passed its first quarter century, the major hope for improvement came from the generation of Iranians who had grown up since 1979 and from their risky reform efforts on behalf of women's rights, social justice, freedom of expression, and other facets of democracy.

By contrast, ancient Egypt, also a theocracy ruled by a supreme religious leader (and one who was regarded as a god) appears to have had a more benign form of government. Although Egypt's society was sharply divided into classes, ranging from farmer/laborer to mighty pharaoh, the governed appear to have been less oppressed. There was also an opportunity for mobility between classes, women had a surprisingly high degree of economic autonomy and social freedom and, through the very dictates of the theocratic system, education, the arts, and the sciences flourished.

In a very different part of the world, neither the modern-day Middle East of Iran nor the ancient Africa of Egypt, a series of theocratic political units with distinctive cultural identities began to emerge in the early centuries following the birth of Christ. They may be said to have begun with the Maya of the so-called Classic Period (250–900 CE) and to have ended with the Aztecs (1325–1521 CE).

The rise and fall of these civilizations took place in that part of the Western Hemisphere that is known as Mesoamerica. This term, as used by archeologists, generally means central and southern Mexico, Mexico's Yucatan Peninsula, Guatemala, and adjoining countries of Central America.

The ancestors of the Mesoamericans were Ice Age nomads from Asia who crossed the frozen land bridge to the Americas, which became the Bering Strait after the ice melted. These first human inhabitants of the American continent probably arrived about 20,000 years ago, eventually fanning out to all parts of North, Central, and South America.

Originally the Maya, who settled primarily in southeastern Mexico, Guatemala, and Honduras, were hunters and gatherers. As the climate warmed, new vegetation sprang up in both the highlands and the lowlands of Mesoamerica. Among the wild grasses of the region were those that would evolve into the maize plant, the source of corn, which would become the staple, along with beans, squash, and chili peppers. The cultivation of the corn plant, which may have begun among the Maya as early as 5000 BCE, made possible a settled agricultural life which, in time, became the basis for the growth of an advanced form of civilization.

Like the ancient Egyptians, the early Maya farming people developed an array of gods who they believed were responsible for the sun, the rain, and the soil that ensured the growth of their crops. To win the favor of these gods, as well as those who presided over other natural phenomena, over birth and death, and over the cosmos and creation—in the case of the Maya and later also the Aztecs—required extreme forms of worship. They included not only self-mutilation, mainly in the form of personal bloodletting, but also the offering of human lives as sacrifices to the gods.

The Maya and the Aztec hierarchies consisted of kings who were considered to be divine and a priesthood that decreed the time and nature of public religious ceremonies, based on the highly developed calendars of these Mesoamerican peoples. Such ceremonies might be held to garner the favor of the gods for agricultural bounty, the health of a new king or heir to the throne, or the success of a military campaign.

In the case of the Maya kings who ruled such individual city-states as Copan in Honduras, Tikal in Guatemala, and Palenque in Mexico (of which there were about sixty during the Classic Period), the main purpose of warfare was seldom to annex the territory of a neighboring city-state. It was rather to secure captives of high rank such as warriors, nobles, and even kings to be offered to the gods as human sacrifices. In general, the city-states of the Maya numbered between 20,000 and 60,000 people, with frequent warfare maintaining a balance of power among them.

The Aztecs, on the other hand, created an empire in central Mexico starting in the 1300s that eventually stretched from the Gulf of Mexico to the Pacific Ocean and that incorporated a number of related but non-Aztec peoples such as the Chichimecs and the Tepanecs. From these groups and others, the Aztecs exacted tribute and booty, as well as lives for the purpose of human sacrifice. By 1519, the time of the Spanish invasion of Mexico by Hernán Cortés, the urban zone of the Aztec Empire, known as Tenochtitlan, had a population of approximately 300,000.

Among both the Maya kings of the city-states and the imperial Aztecs of the vast empire, however, the supreme rulers were seen as responsible for appeasing the gods. In the case of the Maya kings, they and their wives and families frequently engaged in personal bloodletting, piercing their tongues, lips, ears, cheeks, and male organs with stingray spines and often drawing thorned ropes through their wounds. The Maya populace, too, engaged in forms of self-mutilation on the occasion of religious festivals.

Such acts among the Maya are documented in carved stone lintels, in polychrome pottery, and in ceramic figurines that are part of the body of Maya art that has been retrieved from the past.

Human Sacrifice among the Maya and the Aztecs

The Maya city-states that flourished during the Classic Period, starting around 250 CE, went into decline for mysterious reasons by 900. Food shortages, natural disasters, a breakdown in trade, or revolts by the farming and laboring classes against the elite, may have been among the causes. Human sacrifice continued to be practiced, however, among the Late Postclassic Maya on the Yucatan Peninsula, and was described by the Spanish bishop, Diego de Landa, who arrived there in the mid–1500s.

In an eyewitness account, Landa wrote that after the intended victim had been painted blue (the color of sacrifice), he was laid on his back on a stone on the temple platform atop the Maya pyramid. Four men held him down, each one grasping an arm or a leg. "At this time," Landa continued, "the executioner . . . with a knife of stone, and with much skill and cruelty struck him with the knife between the ribs of his left side under the nipple . . . plunged his hand in there and seized the heart."

The still-beating heart was then placed on a plate and given to a priest who smeared the faces of the temple gods with the fresh blood. The corpse might then be cast down to the crowds below. Women and children were also sacrificed in this fashion.

Similarly, the Aztecs also ripped the hearts from the bodies of sacrificial captives on the platforms or steps of their temple-topped pyramids. The practice was seen as a means of offering nourishment to the gods for having made human existence possible. It also served to reinforce the political power of the Aztec rulers. Scenes showing the sacrificial process in detail have been found in Aztec codices, books written or drawn on deerskin or on paper made from the fibrous leaves of the agave plant. Among the many artifacts of Aztec art are large carved stone basins designed to hold hearts and blood.

After the conquest of the Aztecs, Spanish friars who tried to get the Aztec priests to renounce human sacrifice were told the following. "They (the ancestors) said that it is through the sacred spirits that all live . . . that they give us our daily fare and all that we drink, all that we eat. Our sustenance, maize, beans. . . . They we supplicate for water, for rain, with which everything flourishes on earth."

The Aztecs also viewed the flayed skin of sacrifice victims as a symbol of renewal and of life germinating from death. During certain festivals dedicated to the Aztec god known as Xipe Totec (Our Flayed Lord), the priests would drape themselves in the human skins for several days until they had shrunken, dried, and cracked, finally splitting apart so the healthy, living body of the priest would emerge.

The Aztecs required extreme forms of religious worship, including human sacrifice. In this nineteenth century engraving, Aztec priests sacrifice a human heart to the sun.

Among the Aztecs, the rulers offered drops of their royal blood on the occasion of their coronation, at which time they were invested with divine power for the purpose of ensuring the continuity and prosperity of the state. As a semi-deified supreme authority, a new Aztec emperor scaled the Great Pyramid at Tenochtitlan (on the site of present-day Mexico City), where he was given a jaguar's claw with which to prick his calves, arms, and ears. As the Aztec emperor not only administered the state politically but was also commander of the armed forces, he had to be empowered as the pursuer of sacrificial victims. For it was only through never-ending bloodshed that the emperor could maintain the obedience of his subjects and guarantee the favor of the gods. Religion, therefore, dominated the practices and justified the search for human sacrifice victims among both the Maya and the Aztecs.

KINGS AND COMMONERS IN MAYA AND AZTEC SOCIETY

The divine rulers of the Maya and the Aztecs held sway over a sharply stratified society. Close to the top of the hierarchy were the nobles of the royal family, the highest ranked members of the priesthood, and leading civil and military officials. Long-distance traders and merchants of valuable goods, master architects and craftspeople, and the upper echelon of warriors formed an intermediary class. All the rest—farmers, laborers, slaves, and the lower-ranking members of captured enemy people—were commoners.

Rank was distinguished, among other factors, by dress and adornment. Among the Maya, the kings wore quantities of jade jewelry, the skins of jaguars and ocelots, and headdresses fashioned from the long shimmering green-gold tail feathers of the prized quetzal bird from the Guatemalan highlands.

The Aztec rulers were in possession of gold and silver (not found in the Maya areas) from the streams and mines of central Mexico, as well as turquoise and jade. The elite of both peoples wore rings, pendants, ear spools, and lip plugs of bone, shell, and precious materials. The Maya, who filed their front teeth into points, decorated the outer surfaces with inlays of jade mosaics.

By contrast, the commoners among both peoples dressed in the coarse fiber known as henequen and adorned themselves with objects made of clay. Among the Aztecs, even the wearing of cotton cloth was forbidden to commoners. The rights and privileges of the elite included, in addition to wealth and display, palatial living, and the opportunity to have many wives, complete power over those who grew the crops, labored at transport, and built the pyramids with their temples to the gods.

Class mobility was almost nonexistent among the Mesoamericans. As to the role of women, the wives of some of the royal families among the Maya participated in bloodletting ceremonies to win favor with the gods, and occasionally served interim terms as queens when there was a break in the dynasties. Among the Aztecs, there were no women rulers at Tenochtitlan from the time of its founding in the 1300s to its demise in the 1520s. There were, however, Aztec priestesses who took part in the festivals celebrating the female deities connected with the growing of corn. Three corn goddesses existed among the Aztecs. They represented the first tender young maize of the season, the dried seed corn that would be harvested for the following year, and the corn of the fall harvest.

Warfare was common among the Mesoamericans and it, too, was an expression of the theocratic control of the rulers over the commoners who were enlisted in the ranks of the foot soldiers. Only the upper echelon of warriors, most of whom were already of noble birth, had the opportunity to enrich themselves by means of the spoils of war.

Even as the Maya battled their neighbors for sacrificial victims— preferably of sufficiently elevated rank to impress the gods to whom so much was owed—they also engaged on their home turfs in a type of ball game that was symbolic of war. Almost all of the city-states of the Maya Classic Period had ball courts on which such games were fought to the death between groups of players.

The opposing teams consisted of as few as one player each to perhaps as many as eleven on a side. The courts, too, varied in size and design. Some merely had sloping sides, hits against which figured in the scoring, while others had stone rings on the upper walls into which the ball—made of rubber from the cured sap of a local tree—was to be tossed. Such balls could weigh more than five pounds.

An even more challenging factor raised the stakes in the Maya ball game. The players were not permitted to use their hands or feet on the ball. To score a goal point they could only strike the ball with their upper arms, shoulders, waists, hips, or thighs.

The Aztecs, too, engaged in the Mesoamerican ball game, which had been handed down to them from earlier cultures, including those that they had incorporated into their empire. It is believed that the ball games were played for sport, to settle disputes, or to foretell the outcome

guzma. michuacā.

An Aztec drawing depicts the Spanish invaders under Hernán Cortés, who eventually toppled Montezuma II and the Aztec Empire.

of larger battles. There is no question, however, of their seriousness. Ball courts in both the Maya and the Aztec areas have been found to be decorated with skull racks—row upon row of skeletal heads of players who lost their lives attempting to defend their skills in the game of death that was played on the ball courts.

THE LEGACY OF THE MAYA AND AZTEC THEOCRACIES

Nineteenth-century explorers from the United States and Great Britain made the earliest forays into the ancient Maya sites of the Classic Period. These visitors were astonished at the artistic magnificence of the carved stone structures moldering in the tangled vines and roots of the Central American jungles.

In addition to the great plazas with their soaring stepped pyramids and temple platforms, there were carved symbols that appeared to be a form of writing. In time, specialists known as Mayanists began an intensive study of these people. They learned that in addition to their artistic accomplishments, they were remarkably advanced in the sciences.

The Maya had a system of counting that included the concept of zero, which was unknown in Europe at the time. They had a complex dual calendar system that recorded both sacred and civil time, and that meshed with one another. And they understood the heavens beyond the phases of the moon and the solar year. They could also predict eclipses and track the movement of the planets and the stars.

Finally, their written language was discovered to be a highly developed system of hieroglyphics that was painstakingly deciphered by skilled epigraphers. The Maya not only wrote on stone, wood, ceramics, bone, shell, and jade, but also on paper made of fig-tree bark or of deerskin, which was then folded accordion-style into the books, known as codices.

As a result of the many artistic and intellectual achievements of the Maya, Mayanists of the early 1900s viewed them as a gentle, peace-loving people, their peasantry ruled by devout and benevolent priest-kings who did not seek personal grandeur or theocratic overlordship. By the 1960s, however, much new evidence had come to light through carvings and writings that stressed the Maya religious beliefs in terms of their emphasis on both personal bloodletting and human sacrifice.

Similarly, the Aztecs also created impressive art in the form of sculpted stone figures of gods and warriors and sacred animals such as

Montezuma II, The Last Great Aztec Emperor

Montezuma (also called Moctezuma, Motecuhzoma) II took the Aztec throne in the year 1502. The emperor's fate was unlike that of the Classic Period kings of the Maya city-states, whose once-glorious pyramids, temples, and other structures slowly and mysteriously crumbled in the jungles of Guatemala and elsewhere around 900 CE.

On the contrary, Montezuma's domain came crashing to the ground almost thunderously, starting with the invasion of Spanish forces under the leadership of Hernán Cortés in 1519.

No sooner had the Europeans landed on the Gulf Coast of Mexico, a far distance from the urban capital of Tenochtitlan in the central highlands, than the emperor, in a display of his godly power and wealth, sent gifts of gold and silver to the newcomers. Montezuma's pride in his riches, along with the resentment of neighboring peoples from whom he had long been exacting tribute in the form of labor, goods, and human sacrifice victims, contributed to his downfall.

When at last the invaders reached the enormous ceremonial center of Tenochtitlan, they began to realize fully the extent of their prize. The ritual center, which was also the sacred heart of the empire, contained a great four-tiered stepped pyramid that supported temples to the Aztecs' two principal gods, as well as numerous other imposing sites of worship, public buildings, plazas, parade grounds, a ball court, and a skull rack. The latter contained thousands of trophy heads of sacrifice victims.

In the final days of conquest in 1521, Montezuma realized that his efforts at appeasement of the invaders had been a serious mistake. His warriors turned against him, for he was seen as having betrayed the Aztec ideal of divine rulership. One report states that the emperor was stoned to death by his own people in a public demonstration of anger, another that he was secretly strangled. We will never know for sure.

Montezuma's brother was elected to replace him for the brief time that remained before the Aztec Empire fell completely, for the next step was the attack by Cortés on the Great Pyramid. The destruction of its idols and its shrines to the Aztec gods signaled the ultimate defeat of the theocratic state.

Other factors, too, played a role in dismantling the civilization of the Aztecs, as well as other Mesoamerican groups of their time. They included the Aztec practice of ruling by instilling fear in its subjects, faulty Aztec calendrical prophecies that predicted victory rather than defeat, and the superiority of the Spanish arms. In the longer term, the Spanish invasion was also responsible for the annihilation of millions of Mesoamericans as a result of European-introduced diseases such as measles and smallpox to which the populations of the Americas had no resistance.

rattlesnakes, jaguars, and eagles. Other arts and crafts included ritual masks of turquoise mosaic, ceramics, jewelry, and objects such as sacrificial knives carved from obsidian, the hard volcanic glass found in abundance in the central highlands.

Also, like the Maya, the Aztecs were scientifically advanced with regard to the calendar, the cosmos, and writing, and both peoples had their myths of creation that were highly complex and deeply thoughtful. Yet, intellectual pursuits and human artistic genius became subverted in both cultures to the demands of the gods. The Aztecs sprinkled the special foods offered to their deities with drops of human blood, the pyramids of Tenochtitlan ran red with slaughter, and skull racks bore witness to the quantity of human victims.

Ironically, religion, which has the capacity to be ennobling and to lift the human spirit toward the loftiest of goals, became an instrument of death in the Mesoamerican theocracies, including those of the Maya and the Aztecs.

4
A Christian Theocracy: ■ ■ ■
MORMONS IN THE YOUNG UNITED STATES

RELIGIOUS CONVERSION from the belief system of the Aztecs to the Christianity of the Spanish invaders was a principal element in the conquest of the Mesoamericans. In his assault on Tenochtitlan, the Aztec ceremonial center, Cortés captured the Great Pyramid, installing Christian shrines and casting down the images of the Aztec gods from the temples that crowned it. For the Aztecs, the destruction of their holiest site to the accompaniment of gunfire, flames, falling beams, and dying warriors was not only a supremely shocking act, but an act that signaled the death of the Aztec gods and foretold the religious victory of the Christian conquerors.

THE ORIGIN OF CHRISTIANITY
Who were the Christian invaders of the Aztec world and what was their history? At the time of the Spanish invasion, fifteen hundred years had passed since the life on earth of Jesus Christ, who had been born in ancient Israel during the time of the Roman ruler Herod the Great. As Jesus himself left no writings, most of what we know about him appears in the form of written accounts known as Gospels telling of his life, death, and resurrection, as well as his messages and teachings as the prophet of the new religion known as Christianity.

The Gospels, written by followers of Jesus in the decades after his death, which took place in approximately 30 CE, tell us that he was a

Among the innumerable representations of Jesus, the founder of Christianity, is this portrait by the sixteenth century Italian artist Titian.

Jew, as were his early followers. By the year 100, however, communities of Jews and non-Jews who thought of themselves as Christians had already begun to evolve into affiliated groups for the purpose of worship, and these groups began to spread across the Near East and into ancient Greece and Rome.

It was in ancient Rome that the newly formed Christian affiliations, or early church groups, began to be persecuted for their belief in the premise that there was only one God and Father and only one Lord, his Son, Jesus Christ. The religion of the Roman Empire included a number of pagan faiths, and Roman citizens worshipped a pantheon of civilly approved official gods. As a result, the Roman authorities refused to accept the Christian concept of a single deity.

As early as 64 CE, the Roman emperor Nero accused the city's Christians of having started a great fire in Rome, which had been of his own making, and ordered mass executions. The Christians' real crime, as the emperor saw it, was their refusal to worship the state gods. A second flare-up occurred under another Roman emperor toward the end of the first century, but it was not until the second and especially the third centuries that Christian persecution became more widespread.

Events at the start of the fourth century included an effort on the part of the Emperor Diocletian to attempt to restore the ancient gods of Rome as part of a massive religious renewal. As described in John C. Dwyer's *Church History,*

> In 303 Diocletian ordered the destruction of the churches and the burning of the holy books. In the same year, he stripped all Christians of the Empire of their civil rights . . . he ordered the imprisonment of the clergy, with torture and death for those who refused to sacrifice to idols. One year later he extended this decree to all Christians.

Yet, almost on the heels of this most severe of persecutions came the acceptance of Christianity by a succeeding Roman emperor. In the year 313, Constantine I, although not yet a Christian, granted unlimited freedom of religion to all of those dwelling in the Roman Empire. Two years later, Constantine abolished the punishment of crucifixion—the very means by which Jesus had died—and Sunday, the Christian holy

Why Christianity May Have Been Chosen Over Paganism

What, in retrospect, are thought to be some of the reasons for the acceptance of Christian monotheism over the polytheistic beliefs that had previously ruled the Roman populace?

The examples of brotherhood, charity, and compassion displayed by early Christians, as well as their willingness to face martyrdom for their faith, are believed to be among the principal reasons. Christianity also offered moral values with regard to human behavior, including matters of guilt and atonement, and it provided new answers to the eternal questions of death and immortality.

day, was made a legal holiday in 321. The pagan religion of ancient Rome was declared to be a form of false worship two years later, in 323.

The Church of Rome, which later became known as the Roman Catholic Church, had gone from being a scattered and persecuted minority to an established institution composed of a hierarchy of clergy headed by a supreme spiritual ruler with the title of pope.

THE CATHOLIC POPES AND THE PROTESTANT REVOLT

Today, the only theocratic state in the world other than Islamic Iran is the tiny enclave in the city of Rome known as the Vatican. As the home of the pope and the global headquarters of the Roman Catholic Church, this one-hundred-acre territory with its population of approximately one thousand is a religious and administrative center that also functions as a completely sovereign nation and maintains diplomatic relations with numerous countries.

As all of the Vatican's executive, legislative, and judicial powers are under the direct control of its supreme spiritual leader, the pope, this example of a religious state—with its famed Saint Peter's Basilica, palaces, museums, and library—might be called a Catholic theocracy.

The Vatican also, however, represents nearly 2,000 years of papal history, during which time the powers of the papacy as a religious, political, and economic force were extensive. From the early Middle Ages, in the 400s CE, to the Renaissance era of the fifteenth and sixteenth centuries, Europe was dominated by the Roman Catholic faith and by a series of popes who frequently clashed with the emperors, kings, and other rulers of its various countries and political units.

The church provided the faithful with a number of benefits throughout its long reign. During the Middle Ages, it preserved learning through its monasteries and was responsible for the construction of places of worship that included churches and cathedrals of distinction. It also emerged as the patron and the inspiration for the art and architecture of the Renaissance, especially in Italy.

On the other hand, its leadership had in many ways departed from the original teachings of Jesus Christ. The male-dominated church hierarchy had long ago abandoned the regard of Jesus for women as demonstrated in his acts of compassion and social justice. Nor had overbearing political power of the kind appropriated by the organized church been one of the goals of Jesus.

Even more contrary to the teachings of Jesus, who emphasized loving thy neighbor, were such militant and violent events in papal history as the Crusades and the Inquisition. The Crusades, or Holy Wars, of the eleventh to thirteenth centuries were undertaken by European Christians to liberate Jerusalem from its Muslim inhabitants, resulting in looting and slaughter. The Inquisition, particularly the Spanish Inquisition which began in the 1400s, sought to root out false believers and to punish them with various forms of torture.

By the 1500s, the worldly power of the Roman Catholic Church as well as certain practices on the part of the papacy had begun to lead to objections from the faithful. Among these practices were the luxurious lifestyles and moral laxity of members of the church leadership, the buying and selling of sacred offices, and the sale by the church of so-called indulgences—gifts of money made to the church as a means of reducing the penalties for sin.

Principal among those who sought reform was the German Catholic monk Martin Luther, who, on a visit to Rome in 1510, was deeply disturbed by the ostentation he witnessed, much of which was being paid for by Rome's hardworking German subjects.

In 1517 Luther, who believed that only God could forgive the sins of the faithful, summed up the indulgence abuses of the church into ninety-five "theses," or theological statements, which he made public for all to read. The theses were followed a few years later by additional works in which Luther questioned what was essentially the theocratic nature of the papacy. Were the popes divinely endowed and was their authority and their judgment infallible?

Much of the success of Luther's religious movement, which came to be known as the Reformation, was due to the recently developed technology of moveable type, which led to the invention of the printing press by Johann Gutenberg in the mid–1400s. Although Luther was excommunicated by the Roman Catholic Church in 1521, his theories arguing that scripture rather than the papacy was the true word of God, spread among a public that was quickly becoming literate—and could read Luther's translation of the New Testament from Latin into German.

In addition to Germany, the Reformation was well received in Switzerland (where other reformers, including Huldreich Zwingli and John Calvin, preached), in France (where the Calvinists were called Huguenots), in Scandinavia, and in Scotland. In England,

An illustration derived from a glass painting in a church of the Middle Ages shows a fierce battle being fought between Crusaders (on the left) and Muslims, in 1099.

the Reformation began with the quarrel between King Henry VIII and the pope over Henry's demand that he be allowed to divorce his first wife, an act that was strictly forbidden by the Roman Catholic Church.

As the Reformation-born religion known as Protestantism divided itself into numerous denominations, it spread from Europe in the 1500s to almost every corner of the world, including the American colonies and the young United States.

Many of the emerging Protestant groups were instrumental in abolishing the political abuses of older religions. They turned away from the concept of the theocratic state in which the religious leader determined the faith of all the inhabitants. Instead, they tended to foster more democratic forms of government, to promote popular elections, written constitutions, and civil liberties.

Ironically, however, in spite of its revolutionary fervor and its strong reformist spirit, Protestantism also tended in some cases to became as self-righteous and as dictatorial—in other words, as theocratic—as the papacy that it had tried to discredit. It has often been said of the Puritan forefathers of New England that their mission in coming to America was to practice their religion according to their own rules (free of opposition from the Church of England) and to demand that everybody else do the same.

While most Protestant groups in the young United States, such as the Puritans, the Anglicans (Church of England), the Lutherans, and the Calvinists, were of Western European origin, the nation itself was destined to give rise to numerous new denominations springing from the Protestant movement. Today such offshoots of major religious groups are estimated to number in the tens of thousands worldwide, and new subdivisions, or sects, are constantly being developed.

One such new religious offshoot that, with the passage of time, evolved into a leading world faith came into existence in the early nineteenth century in the northeastern United States. Its birth took place during a period of religious revivalism, a ferment that was sweeping New England and upper New York State and was known as the Second Great Awakening. During this time of nationalist fervor, Americans appeared to be looking for their own version of the origin of Christianity, one that might apply directly to their native land and bring Jesus Christ more intimately into their lives.

The name of the new religion was Mormonism. Its adherents were called Mormons or, later and more formally, members of The Church of Jesus Christ of Latter-day Saints. The founder of the religion was Joseph Smith, a fourteen-year-old farm boy who had been born in Vermont on December 23, 1805, and was living, at the time of his first revelation, in the small town of Manchester, New York.

JOSEPH SMITH AND THE BOOK OF MORMON

Joseph Smith was among those who were searching in 1820s rural northeastern America for a true religion, one in which he could drown his faith with confidence. As a result, he sought encounters with holy spirits who might guide him toward making a choice. Smith reported that his first encounter took place in 1820 in a wooded area where a shaft of light revealed the presence of God and Jesus. When Smith questioned the two about which religion was the right one, they replied that all of the existing sects were wrong.

Smith's second visitation from a guiding spirit took place three years later. In 1823, he was approached by an angel named Moroni who told him of a book written on golden plates that he would find buried in the soil of a hill a few miles distant, known as Cumorah.

Apparently awaiting a further sign, Smith began to visit the hill every year until, in 1827, he once again found himself in the presence of Moroni, who gave him the golden plates that he had spoken of four years earlier.

The plates, which Smith was permitted to take home with him, had presumably been buried some 1,400 years earlier and were inscribed in a language that Joseph described as "reformed Egyptian." With the help of a pair of "seeing stones" supplied by the angel Moroni, Joseph Smith was able to translate the golden plates into what became the Book of Mormon, or the Mormon bible.

The angel Moroni was said to have delivered the golden plates of the Book of Mormon to Joseph Smith and witnesses testified to having seen them.

The Story on the Golden Plates

The story inscribed on the golden plates tells of two ancient Hebrew tribes descended from a patriarch named Lehi. Six hundred years before the birth of Christ, Lehi and his family are said to have journeyed by boat to North America. There, Lehi's sons Nephi and Laman quarrel and split into warring factions, with Lehi favoring the Nephites. The Lamanites, who have not obeyed the Lord, are cursed by God and punished with darkened skin, making them the ancestors of the Native Americans, otherwise known as the "red sons of Israel."

The golden plates go on to report that shortly after the death and resurrection of Jesus Christ in Jerusalem, Jesus makes the journey to North America. There, he preaches his gospel to the warring Nephites and Lamanites, and brings them some 200 years of peace and reconciliation, during which time both clans prosper.

After this period, however, the Lamanites backslide into sin and impiety and, in a bloody battle, they kill the Nephite leader whose name is Mormon, along with hundreds of thousands of his followers. Only Moroni, the son of the Nephite general, Mormon, survives to record the history of the Nephites as inscribed on the golden plates buried for 1,400 years on the hill named Cumorah.

Eleven witnesses testified to having seen the golden plates during the time in September 1827 when Joseph Smith had custody of them and was translating them into English with the use of the "seeing stones" (known as the Urim and the Thummim). Eight of the witnesses later said that they had actually "hefted" or held the plates in their hands. Once the translation was completed, however, the angel Moroni had reclaimed the golden plates from Smith and there is no record of their having been seen since.

The method that Joseph Smith used in writing the Book of Mormon was to dictate his translation of the golden plates to one or another friend who served temporarily as a scribe. The two would work in one room with a blanket dividing the space into areas of privacy. By the middle of 1829, the manuscript was ready to be copyrighted and, in March 1830, 5,000 copies had been printed by a small press in Palmyra, New York, and were ready to go on sale. One of Smith's friends, who had also taken dictation from the golden plates, mortgaged his farm to obtain the $3,000 to pay the printer's bill.

The Book of Mormon ran to 588 pages. It incorporated large portions of the Bible as well as the details of the story translated from the golden plates. Believers soon helped establish a church in a log house in the nearby town of Fayette, New York, and began to baptize each other. With each new member serving as a missionary, small congregations began to crop up throughout the area.

It was made clear from the start, however, that Joseph Smith was the prophet and the divine authority of the expanding religion and that the governing of the church and its adherents, as well as new revelations, were to come directly from him. In 1827, Smith had married his sweetheart, Emma Hale, who, in 1830, was given the assignment of putting together a hymnbook for the church.

Joseph also began to compile additional religious works for his homegrown New World faith. He designated North America as the new Holy Land, later naming Independence, Missouri, as the site of the Garden of Eden. One of the reasons for the rapid acceptance of Mormonism was that the Book of Mormon had been produced, unlike the Bible, in an age of literacy. Even more important in bringing converts to the new church was Smith's appearance and personal magnetism. Fawn M. Brodie, one of Smith's biographers, described the onetime vision-seeking farm boy as follows.

> He was big, powerful, and by ordinary standards very handsome, except for his nose, which was aquiline and prominent. His large blue eyes were fringed by fantastically long lashes, which made his gaze seem veiled and slightly mysterious . . . when he was speaking with intense feeling the blood drained from his face, leaving a frightening, almost luminous pallor . . . here was no ordinary man.

Not all of the responses to the new religion and to the story set forth in the Book of Mormon, however, were favorable. In Palmyra, where the book had been printed, a local newspaper, the *Freeman,* suggested that the "golden bible" should be treated "with contempt," while newspapers in the nearby bigger city of Rochester expressed horror and outrage. A review of the Book of Mormon in the *Rochester Daily Advertiser* of April 2, 1830, stated that "A viler imposition was never practiced. It is an evidence of fraud, blasphemy, and credulity, shocking both to Christians and Moralists."

Smith was accused of being a religious imposter who had started out as a sorcerer, a conjurer of spirits, in order to produce revelations that would elevate him to the status of prophet. Members of the more widely practiced religions of the day—many of them stemming from the teachings of John Calvin and from New England Puritanism—saw Smith's Mormonism as a breaking away from the concept of a stern and wrathful God.

Brodie wrote of Joseph Smith,

He believed in the good life, with a moderate self-indulgence in food and drink, occasional sport, and good entertainment. And that he succeeded in enjoying himself to the hilt detracted not at all from the semi-deification with which his own people enshrouded him . . . his theology in the end . . . promised in heaven a continuation of all earthly pleasures—work, wealth, sex, power.

SMITH LEADS THE MORMONS TO OHIO, MISSOURI, AND ILLINOIS

Early in 1831, threatened by a hostile press and an opposing public, Joseph Smith had a divine revelation. He was to gather his flock and leave the region of Palmyra, New York, for the village of Kirtland in northeastern Ohio, where he had already established a small Mormon community through missionaries he had sent out beforehand.

Smith had no difficulty in convincing his followers of the need to leave their homes in New York and to build a new society under his guidance. "The enemy in the secret chambers," he warned, "seeketh your lives." Moreover Smith promised his followers that in obeying his commandment they would be "endowed with power from on high . . . have no laws but my laws . . . for I am your lawgiver, and what can stay my hand?"

Although Kirtland was more hospitable to the followers of "Joseph the Prophet," as Smith announced himself to the local population, there were financial problems from the start. Most of the New York Mormons had had to sell their farms at a loss because of their hasty departure, or rented them out cheaply, or simply left them behind. Smith, however, reminded the newcomers, hard up as they were, that they were not to forget the poorer and needier members in the new Mormon community.

By midsummer of 1831, the migration from New York to Ohio was more or less completed, and there were approximately two thousand devout followers living in Kirtland. Already, though, Joseph Smith had had yet another heavenly revelation. The Missouri frontier was to be the ultimate place of settlement for the Mormons and, in order to pave the way, Smith began sending missionaries to Jackson County, Missouri, to convert the Indians. His revelation had told him that the town of Independence lay at the very heart of the Promised Land. There he would build a new Jerusalem to which Jesus Christ would return.

Between 1831 and 1838, the Mormon population of northwestern Missouri swelled and trouble began to simmer between the newcomers and the older settlers. The Mormons, having originated in New York State, were in favor of the abolition of slavery, while Missouri, which had been admitted to the Union in 1821, was a slaveholding state.

Even more irritating to other Missourians, however, was the arrogance and sense of entitlement to the land that the Mormons displayed. It was also feared that the religiously tight-knit Mormons under the theocratic rule of Joseph Smith would take over the growing frontier towns. For in addition to buying up large tracts of land, they were establishing businesses and threatening to run for public office as sheriffs and magistrates.

As early as 1833 there had been mob violence in the form of beating and stoning, as well as tarring and feathering, by Missouri residents on both sides of the fray. As a result, militias were formed and attacks and counterattacks escalated until, in October 1838, an anti-Mormon mob unleashed its hostility in a killing spree that came to be known as the Haun's Mill Massacre.

Haun's Mill was a Mormon settlement out in the countryside, where a number of families of the faithful had established a farming community and a mill. The unforeseen attack of about 200 armed Missouri militiamen resulted in the deaths of some eighteen Latter-day

Saints, as the Mormons now called themselves, including the elderly and children.

Hatred and persecution of the Saints was now so strongly evident that Joseph Smith was forced to renounce his dream of reestablishing the Holy Land on the Missouri frontier. Once again, the Saints would have to seek a new home.

Why were other Americans so hostile to the Mormons? The fear that Mormons would take economic and political control of growing and neighboring communities in the young United States was one of the reasons. It was also apparent that, among the inhabitants of the expanding nation, there was a desire for freedom of expression in social, cultural, and religious matters. Such freedoms were not consistent with the authoritarian restrictions that Smith imposed on his Mormon followers.

While the majority of Americans were churchgoers, they were citizens of a democracy that based its executive, legal, and judicial system on the separation of church and state. Instinctively, most of the Mormons' neighbors shied away from the absolutism and theocratic rule that Smith had established over his flock.

The next stop for the Mormons took them geographically back toward the East, into the state of Illinois. Although the unsettled West beckoned (and would eventually become the home of the Latter-day Saints), Smith chose to lead his people to a largely uninhabited swampland on a bend of the Mississippi River. In that part of Illinois, land was cheap and could be purchased on credit, and other settlers hostile to the Mormon concepts and to their form of local government were relatively few in number.

At least 8,000 Mormons had been forced to leave Missouri following the Haun's Mill Massacre. Also Smith had spent several months in a Missouri jail and he was determined that the persecution the Saints had endured should be well publicized.

Always skilled at using the press, the Mormons published eyewitness accounts of the atrocity and sent them to major American newspapers.

The *Chicago Democrat* of March 25, 1840, noted that the Mormons might well be called "martyr-mongers" and predicted "let Illinois repeat the bloody tragedies of Missouri . . . and the Mormon religion will not only be known throughout the land, but will be very extensively embraced."

Joseph Smith had also been adept from the start at sending out missionaries to bring converts to the new Mormon settlements. To grow the young city on the shore of the Mississippi, which he named Nauvoo, he dispatched Mormon apostles to England. Preaching the superiority of life in America, as well as the gospel of Mormonism, Smith's missionaries were soon successful at increasing the population of Nauvoo by more than a thousand English immigrants each year.

Joseph Smith's control of Nauvoo was that of a theocratic ruler in charge of a small kingdom or, more accurately, a city-state. As described in Richard N. Ostling's *Mormon America,* "Nauvoo's charter provided for no effective separation of powers. . . . The mayor [Smith] served on the city council and was also chief justice of the municipal court."

As the Mormon church was involved in all aspects of government, "civic and religious power overlapped, and the newborn city functioned effectively as an independent theocracy within Illinois . . . there was no separation of church and state of the sort envisioned in the U.S. Constitution."

Wary of the threat of attacks against Nauvoo from hostile and well-armed neighbors, as had happened in Missouri, Smith demanded that the city be allowed to have its own militia. He formed the Nauvoo Legion, a uniformed military corps consisting of 3,000 to 4,000 men.

Although the early years in Nauvoo, 1839 and 1840, were plagued with outbreaks of malaria and cholera, emanating from the undrained swamplands and killing hundreds of inhabitants, the new Land of Zion soon began to prosper. By 1844, Nauvoo had a population of 12,000 to 15,000 Saints, an impressive temple had been built, and Joseph Smith had proudly declared himself to be "King, Priest and Ruler over Israel on Earth."

THE MORMON LEADER HAS A FATEFUL REVELATION IN NAUVOO

As the leader of a new religion that, unlike many others of its time, had succeeded in taking root in American soil, Joseph Smith continued to have revelations that helped to bond Mormonism to God and to eternal life.

In 1841, Smith came upon the concept of baptism of the dead. The ancestors of living Mormons who had had no opportunity to espouse the religion prior to its birth in 1830 could be baptized into the church by proxy. At first, Nauvoo Saints who wanted to grant their forebears the chance to become Mormons in the afterlife underwent the ceremony of vicarious baptism in the Mississippi River. Later the proxy baptisms were held in Mormon temples. Thus departed loved ones could attain salvation by becoming enshrined forever in the Mormon religion.

As a result of an 1842 revelation, Joseph Smith introduced a ritual known as the "endowment," by means of which male church members underwent a ceremony of washing and anointing. They were then dressed in a special undergarment, which had the power to ward off evil, as a form of initiation into the faith. A year or so later, Smith granted Mormon women the privilege of undergoing the initiation ceremony as well. Men attended to men and women attended to women in performing the endowment.

The status of women among the Saints appeared, in the 1840s, to be similar to that of women everywhere in the young United States. While their lives were devoted mainly to childbearing and household duties and they could not vote, hold religious or public office, or serve as missionaries, they were considered to be on a relatively equal footing with men before God

Beneath the surface, however, the Mormon leader had long been wrestling with the subject of monogamy (marriage between one husband and one wife) and polygyny (a form of polygamy in which a husband has more than one wife at the same time) or, as Joseph Smith termed it, "plural marriage."

As early as his days in Kirtland, Ohio, in 1831, Joseph—although still married to Emma—had been tempted in the direction of extramarital activity. As Brodie wrote,

> Monogamy seemed to him—as it has to many men who have not ceased to love their wives, but who have grown weary of marital exclusiveness—an intolerably circumscribed way of life. . . . But Joseph was no careless libertine who could be content with clandestine mistresses. There was too much of the Puritan in him, and he could not rest until he had redefined the nature of sin and erected a stupendous theological edifice to support his new theories on marriage.

With the widespread acceptance of his most recent revelation—God's commandment that the Saints practice plural marriage—Joseph Smith began to make plans to extend his theocratic rule beyond Nauvoo. Why not run for president of the United States in the national election of 1844 and thus establish the kingdom of God on earth?

Smith considered the leading presidential candidates to be as indifferent to God as they were to Mormonism, and he advocated a form of government for the United States that he called a "theodemocracy." Writing in the Mormon newspaper, the *Nauvoo Neighbor*, of April 17, 1844, Smith declared, "There is not a nation or a dynasty now occupying the earth which acknowledges Almighty God as their lawgiver."

Nor did Smith approve of the multiparty system that was the basis of American democracy. He favored a one-party state headed by a president-dictator, with powers similar to those of the mayor of Nauvoo, where Smith was also head of the church, lawmaker and judge, leading business owner and real-estate mogul, chief of the Nauvoo Legion military force, and the husband of possibly close to fifty wives.

It was over the issue of polygamy that Joseph Smith was destined to tumble from the lofty position he occupied as the leader of the Saints. A church official named William Law, who had served as second-in-command to Smith, began to raise objections to the growing practice of plural marriage.

When Smith and Law could no longer come to terms, Law acquired a printing press and on June 7, 1844, issued a newspaper called the *Nauvoo Expositor*. In his publication, Law not only denounced polygamy (with examples and the sworn testimony of witnesses) but also attacked Smith's attempt to unite church and state.

"We do not believe," Law wrote in the *Expositor*, "that God ever raised up a Prophet to christianize a world by political schemes and intrigue. . . . We will not acknowledge any man as king or law-giver to the church: for Christ is our only king and law-giver."

Smith was furious when the *Expositor* came off the press and was distributed in the nearby non-Mormon localities of Warsaw and Carthage, where hostility to Smith, his authoritarian rule, and his militant Nauvoo Legion had been growing for some time. As polygamy was illegal in the state of Illinois, Smith vehemently denied that it existed (the Mormon church would not admit to polygamy until 1852, by which time the majority of the Saints were living in Utah).

As a result, Smith accused Law of libel. On June 10, 1844, he called a meeting of the Nauvoo City Council and got a unanimous vote to immediately smash Law's press and destroy all existing copies of the *Expositor*. Completely outnumbered in Nauvoo and fearing for his life, Law had little choice but to flee the city with his family.

The governor of Illinois, Thomas Ford, now stepped into the

Joseph Smith's Revelation on Polygamy

On July 12, 1843, Joseph Smith recorded in a journal known as *The Doctrine and Covenants* that he had received a commandment from God formally endorsing plural marriage in the Mormon church.

To Joseph, this commandment from God seemed to him justified for several reasons. For one thing, he had searched the Old Testament and found many instances of polygamous marriage among its powerful male figures. Already, according to Joseph's 1841 revelation regarding the baptism of the dead, it was possible for a man who had been widowed and who had remarried to have two or even more wives in heaven, so why not on earth?

In addition, plural marriage ensured that no young woman who had become involved with a married man would be abandoned and forced to become a prostitute. And any children resulting from the relationship would be cared for in the polygamous household rather than becoming fatherless.

At first, Smith shared his revelation concerning plural marriage with only a few of his closest friends and church officials among the Saints. Emma, Joseph's wife of sixteen years, was not, however, taken into his confidence. When she learned of the new commandment, she was deeply upset and, even after Joseph began to practice polygamy more openly than in his hidden past, she remained in denial.

There were many Mormon women, though, who did not object to

becoming the added-on wives of married men. Some of the unmarried females were still in their teens, while others were widows or spinsters, flattered to be sought after by powerful church leaders and ready to fulfill the commandment guaranteeing eternal wedlock.

All in all, Smith is believed to have had at least thirty-three and as many as forty-eight wives, including Emma, who remained with him to the end in spite of her disapproval and the hurt she endured.

picture, for the non-Mormons were pressuring him to call up the state militia against Smith, who on June 18 had mobilized the Nauvoo Legion. Fearing a civil war on the western border of his state, Ford ordered Smith to give himself up to face trial.

In a panic, Joseph Smith, accompanied by his brother Hyrum and two other loyal supporters, chose to flee, sailing across the Mississippi to the Iowa Territory in a small boat on the stormy night of June 22. After lodging briefly with some Saints who had settled in the Territory, Joseph received a note from Emma begging him to return and face charges, for Nauvoo was now without a leader and the city was in jeopardy.

On June 24, Joseph was rowed back across the river and taken to jail in Carthage, the county seat. Governor Ford was determined that Smith and his supporters should receive a fair trial. The jailer was so lax that Saints who visited Joseph and Hyrum in their cell managed to smuggle in two guns for the brothers.

None of these advantages were of any use. Around five o'clock on the afternoon of June 27, a hate-crazed mob of about 125 militiamen and local citizens from the anti-Mormon town of Warsaw, their faces blackened with gunpowder, stormed the two-story jail building.

Joseph and Hyrum had been moved to the upper floor for their own protection. The attackers, however, swarmed up the stairs and into the room firing their weapons. The brothers tried to defend themselves with the smuggled guns, but they were clearly outnumbered. Hyrum was killed instantly. Joseph, apparently not yet shot, tried to jump from the window.

The next moment he was hit from behind as well as from the ground below, and tumbled to the earth, dead. Joseph Smith was thirty-eight years old. He had never named a successor, but another theocratic leader was waiting in the wings to lead the Saints to their destiny in the American West.

THE WAY WEST

If Joseph Smith was the visionary and the prophet responsible for the birth of the Church of Jesus Christ of Latter-day Saints, Brigham Young, his successor, was the pragmatic, determined, and disciplined leader who would save the foundering inhabitants of Nauvoo, Illinois.

Like Smith, Young was born in Vermont and raised in New York State. He was baptized into the Mormon church in 1832, at the age of thirty-one, and became a missionary, recruiting converts from Canada and England. He had earlier served as president of the twelve apostles of the church.

In 1846, less than two years after Smith's death, Young launched a great 1,300-mile exodus into the valley of the Great Salt Lake in a wilderness that still belonged to Mexico. After the Mexican War, which ended in 1848, the Saints' new home became known (in 1850) as the Utah Territory, with Brigham Young as governor.

Like Smith, Young espoused polygamy and he defied the United States government, allowing girls as young as fourteen to become plural wives. Young is believed to have had nearly thirty to perhaps more than fifty wives, and something like fifty-seven offspring. He commanded that the faithful follow his example, one obvious reason being the production of large families to guarantee the spread of Mormonism. Also, like Smith, Young established a theocratic dictatorship in the Utah Territory, controlling the legislature and the courts through his unification of state and church.

The reputation of Young's governorship of the Utah Territory was irrevocably damaged by the notorious Mountain Meadows Massacre of 1857, in which a contingent of Mormons disguising themselves as Paiute Indians (who also participated in the raid) murdered 120 members of a non-Mormon wagon train heading from Arkansas to California.

The dead included women and children. The federal government held Young, as religious and political leader of the rapidly expanding Utah Mormon community, responsible for the massacre, which was especially brutal. It took until 1877, however, before a culprit was put forward and executed for the crime. He was John D. Lee, a loyal supporter of both Smith and later of Young.

On August 29, 1877, a few months after Lee's execution by a federal firing squad, Young died of blood poisoning from a ruptured appendix. At the time of Young's death, the Mormon church in the Utah Territory boasted a membership of 135,000.

Because many Saints continued to follow the "principle" of polygamy dictated by Smith and Young, Utah was denied statehood until 1896, six years after the 1890 announcement of the then president of the church that there would be an official end to the practice. "As one might expect of any change to such a deep-seated principle," writes Richard N. Ostling in his book *Mormon America*,

" the declaration did not immediately stick. For more than a decade some leaders in the Mormon hierarchy quietly continued to add polygamous wives."

Today the Church of Jesus Christ of Latter-day Saints, which is headquartered in Salt Lake City, Utah, is one of the fastest-growing religions on earth. It has 5.5 million members in the United States and totals 12 million adherents worldwide. The 1978 lifting of a ban on giving full membership status to people of African descent accounts for the expansion of the faith in Africa. Church teaching, however, still forbids interracial marriages between blacks and whites.

The worldwide recruitment of converts continues with as many as 60,000 young men in their late teens or early twenties serving as missionaries for two-year stints. Women may also go out into the field provided they have reached the age of twenty-one and are not yet married.

Emphasis on family life, devotion to religious duties and church activities (including tithing—the contribution of at least 10 percent of gross income), industriousness, and education are the hallmarks of mainstream Mormonism today.

Mormon-sponsored Brigham Young University in Provo, Utah, is the largest religious school of higher education in the United States.

Also, church-affiliated newspapers, radio, and TV disseminate Mormon culture and beliefs to the population of Utah (which is 63 percent Mormon) as well as other major centers of the faith. Nor is it surprising that Mormons fill most elective offices in the state and also make up most of the Utah delegation to the United States Congress.

The spiritual leader of the Mormon church today is given the secular-sounding title of "President." However, he is still considered to be in direct communication with God, and is also referred to as "Prophet, Seer, and Revelator." Yet, there is a major difference between now and the days of theocratic leader Joseph Smith.

Smith tried for the most part to dominate the majority by imposing minority rule on them, reaping fear, hostility, and violence. Today the democratic principles of "majority rule, minority rights" appear to be in operation. The vast Mormon successes in politics, business, culture—and of course the expansion of the faith—have come about by dint of sheer numbers.

If there is a downside to the power and prosperity of the Mormon

Mormon polygamist Tom Green, with his five wives and [some of his] twenty-nine children, who went on trial in Utah in 2001. In 2006, long-sought Mormon fundamentalist and polygamist Warren Jeffs was finally captured and faced trial.

church today and to its teaching of family values at their most high-minded and pristine, it is the widely lingering practice of polygamy among Saints who, for the most part, refer to themselves as Mormon Fundamentalists. Estimates of present-day polygamous Mormons run from 40,000 to 100,000. They are scattered through Utah but have also formed communities in Idaho, Nevada, Colorado, Arizona, and California, as well as in Canada and Mexico.

Mormon Fundamentalists refuse to accept the official church's 1890 ban on polygamy. They refute the right of the church to have revoked Joseph Smith's 1843 divine revelation commanding that the Saints practice plural marriage. Nor can they forget that the practice was further endorsed by Brigham Young with the threatening words, "If any of you will deny the plurality of wives, and continue to do so, I promise that you will be damned."

Unhappily, not all polygamous families care for their many offspring. As a result, ill-treated or abandoned children may have to be cared for with public funds, a practice that is often accompanied by welfare fraud. Also, cases of girls and young women who have been abducted to become the plural wives of Mormon men surface from time to time in the press and on radio and TV.

Yet, Mormon Fundamentalists, who are in violation of state laws as well as current church law, cling to the belief that sometimes one must disobey a lesser law to keep a higher one. Polygamy, with its anti-feminist aspects and implications, is probably the principal negative legacy of the theocratic rule of Mormonism's founder, Joseph Smith.

A Taliban Theocracy: **5 ■ ■ ■**
AFGHANISTAN IN THE 1990s

OVER AND OVER, one of the main characteristics of political systems governed by religious fundamentalists appears to be the oppression of women. Among contemporary Muslim nations, Iran—under extremist Shiite rule—offers an example of the restrictions placed on the dress and behavior, as well as the public, social, and personal life, of women throughout the nation.

Yet, as severe as the theocratic leadership of Iran continues to be, it has been unable to restrain the thirst for higher education among its young people, with women currently making up 65 percent of university entrants.

The traditions in Iranian history under dictatorial, but also more reformist, rulers are, in part, responsible for the current ferment that may one day succeed in overthrowing the Shia fundamentalist government of the Islamic Republic of Iran.

Iran's neighboring nation to the east, Afghanistan, has also had a checkered history. Like Iran, it is a Muslim nation that embraced Islam in the 600s, but its population is roughly 80 percent Sunni and only 20 percent Shia, and there are many pre-Islamic tribal beliefs. Also, its extensive desert-like mountainous terrain interspersed with occasional fertile valleys has broken the country into isolated localities and prevented the unification of political, social, and cultural points of view.

Afghan women, forced to wear the burka under Taliban rule, may still be seen in this traditional body-concealing garment as they vote in a post-Taliban election.

After centuries of having been occupied or crisscrossed by Persians, Turks, or Mongols, the Afghans tried to put their own tribal leaders on the throne, only to become embroiled during the 1800s in the British/Russian competition for control of their country.

Independence came at last in 1919, with the Afghan king Amanullah Khan ascending the throne and attempting reforms and modernization. He introduced Western dress and coeducational classes in the schools. While the inhabitants of Kabul, the capital, and other cities favored these changes, tribal and religious elements in the hinterlands rebelled, and he was overthrown and exiled in 1929.

Amanullah Khan's major successor, Zahir Shah, managed to hold onto the throne for forty years, from 1933 to 1973, during which the conflict between reform efforts and Islamic revolts, as well as tribal rivalries, escalated into a state of chaos and instability.

Among the discordant groups seeking political control in Afghanistan in the 1970s there were those who favored modernization modeled not on the United States and western Europe, but on the communist regime of the Soviet Union. Afghanistan's leadership in the late 1970s played Washington and Moscow against each other. The Afghan communist party won out and, in 1979, the Soviets invaded Afghanistan, partly at the behest of its Marxist reformists.

Although Afghanistan's population, especially in the rural areas, was steeped in Islamic law and was far from ready for secular reforms such as literacy for girls, free choice in marriage for women, and the teaching of Marxism, the Soviets continued their occupation for ten years, until 1989. As many as six million Afghans fled the country, taking refuge mainly in neighboring Pakistan or Iran.

During that time, the United States sent aid to Afghanistan in an attempt to drive out its Cold War archenemy. Also, within Afghanistan, guerrilla fighters known as *mujahedeen*, or holy warriors, rose up against the occupiers. Although their commitment to Islam ranged from moderate to extreme and they represented a variety of political agendas, they were united as a rebel force against the Soviets.

Success in ousting the Soviet Union in 1989 was due not only to the guerrilla warfare of the mujahedeen and the military and humanitarian aid received from the United States. There were also growing political and economic problems inside the Soviet Union (which was destined to break apart in 1991), and the occupation of Afghanistan had proven to be costly and unproductive.

With the withdrawal of the Soviets the country seemed open for a new approach toward a government that could perhaps accommodate both Islam and aspects of modernity and reform including education—in a country that was three-quarters illiterate—plus much-needed improvements in health care, infrastructure, and employment.

Finally given their chance, the mujahedeen took control of Kabul and attempted to form a new government for the fractured nation. During the Soviet occupation the contrast between life in the capital and in the rural areas had become increasingly sharp.

In Kabul, where many new government jobs had been created under the Soviets, women went to work in offices wearing short skirts and heels, while in the villages no Afghan woman appeared in public without the enveloping covering of the burka. This garment, usually blue, covered not only the hair and entire body from the neck down, but also the face of the wearer, who was forced to peer at the world through a latticework grille of heavy fabric.

Was there any way that the new interim government—made up of factions that fought constantly among themselves—could reconcile these extremes as well as improve conditions in the war-torn nation that was already the fourth or fifth poorest in the world?

THE COMING OF THE TALIBAN

It was during this era of turmoil in Afghanistan that a new and deeply religious Islamic movement arose and quickly came to the forefront on the military and political scene.

Its members were known as the Taliban, meaning "students of Islam," and they originated in the rural and most conservative parts of the country under the leadership of tribal and village elders.

The Afghans who joined the Taliban had been highly critical of the reformist trends of the Afghan kings, to say nothing of the ten years during which the godless Soviets had been in control of their country. Nor did they feel that the mujahedeen represented Islam in its pure state. On the contrary, they viewed them as politically corrupt and unforgivably lax in the observance of their faith.

Like most revivalist religious movements, the Taliban had a supreme spiritual leader. He was Mullah Mohammed Omar, the term *mullah* meaning a giver of knowledge. Like many of his student followers, Mohammed Omar was a Sunni Muslim from the region around the city of Kandahar in the south.

In 1994, after having fought a *jihad*, or holy war, against the Soviets and then ousting the local warlords and the mujahedeen, the Taliban captured the city of Kandahar, the first of their successful exploits with the Koran and the gun.

The following year, in the words of Mullah Omar, the "simple band of dedicated youths determined to establish the laws of God on Earth" took the city of Herat in western Afghanistan and, in 1996, Jalalabad and Kabul in the east.

The Taliban now had control of two-thirds of the country and were determined to take the rest of it. Still grappling for total control in September 2001, Mohammed Omar declared, "The Taliban will fight until there is no blood in Afghanistan left to be shed and Islam becomes a way of life for our people."

As justification for his theocratic rulership of Afghanistan, in all its severe and dictatorial aspects, Mullah Omar claimed that Allah had appeared to him in human form in a dream.

In the dream, God had commanded him to lead the Taliban to victory over, first, the invading Soviets, then the squabbling mujahedeen, and finally the Northern Alliance—the military force that was blocking him from taking full control of Afghanistan.

The military leader of the Northern Alliance was the popular and charismatic Ahmed Shah Massoud. Like Mullah Omar, who had lost an eye to exploding shrapnel during a battle with the Soviets, Massoud had also led a campaign against the communist occupiers. In fact, Massoud was the most celebrated of the guerrilla leaders during the 1980s and had had the backing of the United States.

In spite of having at one time fiercely opposed a common enemy, the fighters of Massoud's Northern Alliance and the Taliban of Mullah Omar were now, in the late 1990s, bitter enemies after the fall of Kabul. Tribal and ethnic differences also separated the two leaders.

Mullah Omar and the Taliban, almost all of whom had originated in the south, were Pashtuns, a group that made up 40 percent of Afghanistan's population. Massoud's people, on the other hand, were mainly Tajiks, the largest ethnic group in the north and about 25 percent of the population.

Massoud's victories against the Soviets should have ensured him and Afghanistan generous military and humanitarian support from the United States, even after the Soviet Union was forced to withdraw

The Taliban Way of Life

Sharia, or fundamental Islamic law based on the teachings of the Prophet Muhammad, formed the guiding principles of the Taliban. On taking the capital city of Kabul, the new theocratic rulers of Afghanistan broadcast sixteen decrees on the radio, said to have been divinely inspired by the founder of Islam.

In addition to strict rules for dress and behavior among women, and dress and beard requirements for men, there were prohibitions against many recreational activities that were regularly indulged in among the Afghan populace. These included music and dancing, even at weddings, gambling and kite flying, the rearing of homing pigeons, and the playing of drums.

The Islamic prohibition against pictures or other representations of the human or animal form meant that there were to be no movies, TV, or Internet, no photographs in books, magazines, or newspapers, or on packaged products. Sculpted objects in the Kabul Museum were smashed and, in March 2001, the Taliban blew up two enormous ancient statues of Buddha in central Afghanistan, in defiance of wide-ranging pleas from art curators and historians, religious figures, and government leaders around the world.

In addition to wearing the burka when outside their homes, women were to sit at the back of the bus and in the trunk of a taxi if men were in the back seat. They were not to wash clothes in the river or to have their clothing sewn by male tailors. Men were instructed to stop shaving and to grow a beard that was the length of a clenched fist.

Western garments and long hair styles for men were forbidden. The compulsory garment for men was the *shalwar kameez,* a tunic that fell below the knees worn over trousers that covered the ankles. Afghan men with beards or trousers that were too short were subject to arrest.

The punishments for not observing the dictates of the Taliban followed those of Sharia law, and were carried out by the Department for the Promotion of Virtue and the Extermination of Sin (or the Prevention of Vice), also called the Ministry of Morality, through its foot soldiers known as the religious police.

Each violation had its own penalty. For drinking alcohol, one received eighty lashes. Persons who were arrested could expect to receive beatings in prison with canes and thick braided ropes. Women who had worn makeup under their burkas or gone to the market alone and bought items from male vendors were subject to arrest. They were draped in a sheet while being flogged.

Women who were accused of adultery were stoned to death. The traditional penalty for theft was to have one's hand chopped off.

from the country. However, as is all too often the case in international affairs, the United States proved to be both lacking in good foreign intelligence and shortsighted with regard to political and military trends.

The only countries to recognize the Taliban as the legitimate government of Afghanistan were Saudi Arabia, Pakistan, and the United Arab Emirates. As for the United States, neither the CIA (Central Intelligence Agency) nor the State Department had had any sort of meaningful representation in that country after the Soviets left, and the United States Embassy in Kabul had been closed for security reasons since the latter part of 1988.

It was largely as a result of neglect on the part of the United States that the door had been left wide open in Afghanistan for the rising power of the Taliban. U.S. indifference had also made this politically chaotic, war-torn, and impoverished country inviting to the rebellious son of a wealthy Saudi businessman who was seeking a place of refuge from which to conduct acts of terrorism.

Arriving in May 1996, accompanied by his following of Islamic extremists, the Saudi exile settled down initially in Jalalabad at the eastern edge of the country, where he had connections with some of the local warlords. Later he would move to the rugged southeastern portion of Afghanistan, where it was possible to hide out in natural caves and to set up secret training grounds for terrorists. His name was Osama bin Laden.

OSAMA BIN LADEN, THE TALIBAN, AND THE UNITED STATES

Osama bin Laden and the Taliban were made for each other. Although their political linkage was tenuous at first, they shared the severe puritanical views of fundamentalist Islam, were dedicated to the principle of jihad, or holy war, by military and violent means, and were engaged in battling the same enemy—the nations of the West and particularly the United States.

Bin Laden, born in 1957, was one of fifty or more children of a billionaire Muslim contractor who built roads, airports, palaces, and mosques for the oil-rich Saudi rulers. Although well educated and independently wealthy, as were many of his brothers, bin Laden took exception to the presence of American troops, stationed, for purposes of protection and training, on Saudi soil.

Because of his deep religious faith, he demanded that the Saudi

Arabian government remove the "infidels" from the land that had been the birthplace of Islam and was home to its two holiest cities, Mecca and Medina. When it became evident that the Americans would not be asked to leave due to interests linking his country and the United States, bin Laden moved to the Sudan and, after a four-year stay, to Afghanistan, which was a more protected setting for his covert operations.

Shortly after his arrival in Afghanistan, bin Laden had begun to make vindictive and threatening statements about Americans. Whether they were military personnel or innocent civilians, bin Laden declared that all were targets.

He also outlined his reasons for planning attacks on Americans. They included the continued U.S. military and civilian presence in Saudi Arabia, America's friendship with Israel, and its "arrogance and haughtiness" as the "leader of the new world order." For all of these reasons and more, he had declared holy war on the United States and its people.

As early as the mid-1990s, it was discovered that a 1993 attempt to destroy New York City's World Trade Center (in which six people died and over 1,000 were injured) was traceable to the terror network, known as Al Qaeda, operated by bin Laden.

Bombings of American military installations in Saudi Arabia followed, as did the carefully coordinated and violent explosions that simultaneously destroyed two U.S. embassies in Kenya and Tanzania, in East Africa, in 1998. Over 200 died and more than 4,000 were injured, but bin Laden fell short of his goal as only twelve were Americans and the rest East Africans.

In October 2000, bin Laden made yet another foray against America when he sponsored an attack on the U.S. destroyer, the *Cole*, as it lay at anchor off the coast of Yemen at the tip of the Arabian Peninsula. In a suicide bombing, a small craft loaded with explosives seriously damaged the steel-hulled ship, killing seventeen Americans and injuring thirty-nine.

No fanatical suicide mission or act of terrorism, however, approached the assault on the United States that Osama bin Laden had planned for two or more years and that was carried out on September 11, 2001. In the morning hours of an ordinary Tuesday in late summer, four American passenger flights out of airports in Boston, Washington, and Newark were hijacked by nineteen members of bin Laden's Al Qaeda.

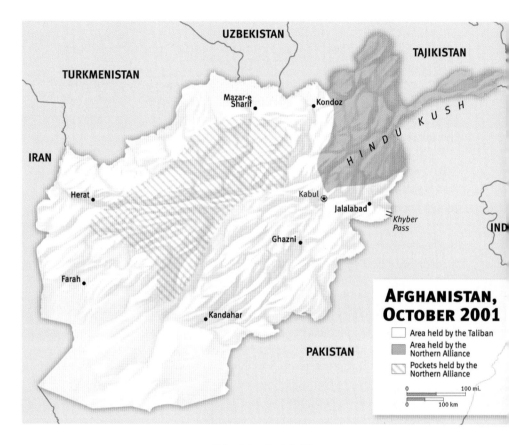

Afghanistan, Post-9/11

The airplanes, laden with fuel, were to be used as flying bombs for the destruction of major targets in New York City and Washington. Three of them hit their mark, two bringing down the twin towers of the World Trade Center in New York and one crashing into a portion of the Pentagon in Washington. The fourth plane, possibly targeted to destroy the White House or the Capitol, was diverted and crashed into a field in Pennsylvania.

The operation was the worst attack on U.S. soil in the nation's history, comparable only to Pearl Harbor, on December 7, 1941. The total loss of life resulting from Osama bin Laden's act of vengeance against his number one enemy was nearly 3,000. How would the United States react? What methods would it use to wage an effective war in Afghanistan, one that would apprehend the stealthy and evasive bin Laden and simultaneously topple the Taliban who were sheltering him?

On September 9, 2001, two days before the 9/11 attack on the United States, agents of bin Laden's Al Qaeda terror network had assassinated the guerrilla fighter, leader of the Northern Alliance, and longtime enemy of the Taliban, Ahmed Shah Massoud. Was bin Laden paving the way for a leaderless Northern Alliance when the United States counterattacked, as he knew it would? It seemed obvious that that was his intention.

The United States' response was not long in coming. On October 7, 2001, President George W. Bush ordered the first military attack on Afghanistan. In a departure from conventional warfare, however, the United States chose not to put troops on the ground at first but to fight a long-distance war with cruise missiles and air strikes. Meantime the Northern Alliance struggled with the rugged terrain in an effort to move south against the Taliban forces, which were well-equipped by bin Laden with tanks, guns, and anti-aircraft weapons.

Although American ground troops did eventually lend support, leading to the Taliban being driven first from Kabul and then from Kandahar, the pursuit of bin Laden and the retreating Taliban was never carried out militarily. The Taliban government in the Afghan capital and in major cities was unseated within two months of the American retaliation for 9/11, but pockets of Taliban resistance remain to the present day. Nor has bin Laden, who is thought to be hiding out in the wild region between southeast Afghanistan and northwest Pakistan—and who surfaces from time to time on Arab television—been apprehended.

AFGHANISTAN TODAY: FROM THEOCRACY TO DEMOCRACY?

Could a country steeped in centuries of antidemocratic tribal and religious law, and resistant to all previous attempts at reform and modernization, change its cultural patterns, its economy, and its political system?

Assuming that the transformation from a Taliban theocracy to U.S. style democracy might be possible in the course of time, Afghanistan has numerous obstacles that would have to be overcome. They include poverty, adult illiteracy, lack of education and health care, the low status of women, and the need for safe and secure roads and highways to reach remote parts of the country.

According to the United Nations, Afghanistan in 2004 ranked 173 out of 178 countries in terms of human development and living standards, making it vulnerable to a return to chaos if its social and economic problems were not addressed. Only 28.7 percent of Afghan adults could read and write, the country's secular educational system was just beginning to be developed, and the average life expectancy was about forty-five.

While more than 50 percent of school-age children were enrolled in classes, girls in rural communities and even in the cities are still often withdrawn from school when they reach puberty. According to tradition, religious families feel it is their duty to see to it that their daughters are sheltered from contact with unrelated males until marriages can be arranged for them.

The annual per capita income of Afghans in 2005 was only $190, and there was an unemployment rate of 25 percent. Fifty-three percent of Afghans were living on less than $1 a day, and the gap between the poorest and the wealthiest members of society was growing.

In spite of all the drawbacks of life in Afghanistan after the fall of the Taliban theocracy in 2001, an attempt was made, with the help of the United States, to install a more enlightened political system.

A first step toward establishing a stable and representative form of government, such as the country had never known before, was taken in June 2002, when a traditional grand council of some 1,600 delegates, known as a *loya jirga,* met in Kabul. Its purpose was to select a president for the country. The man chosen was Hamid Karzai, who had already served as an interim leader for six months.

As Karzai's selection by the *loya jirga* delegates did not represent votes cast by all eligible Afghans, a national election was held more than two years later, in October 2004. Was the country ready for such a process? How would registration and voting places be set up and secured from disruptions by Taliban guerrillas and disgruntled warlords? How would women who lived in remote areas and were still restrained by tradition and by religion from traveling reach the voting centers?

On the plus side, an estimated 10 million Afghans registered to vote in the national election for president. More than 40 percent were said to be women and, with the protection of troops from the United States and other cooperating nations, the election of October 9 was carried out without major incident.

Karzai, who was one of eighteen candidates and who was reportedly favored by the United States, won out over his opponents. There remained, however, much more to be done than the election to a five-year term of a president who had often been called "the mayor of Kabul" because of threats to his life and the need for American protection, especially when traveling outside the capital.

The next step in the democratizing of Afghanistan was that of electing a parliament. Voting took place in September 2005. No political parties had yet been formed and each of the candidates—who included women and Afghans from many ethnic groups—ran as an individual. Voters dipped their fingers into indelible purple ink to avoid anybody voting more than once, and it was believed that half, or a little less, of the population participated.

It was hoped that as a result of the election of a parliament, Afghan citizens would be able to take their grievances against the central government to their local elected representatives, instead of depending on the armies of local warlords or rogue militias for the basic problem of security. In addition, the new government was responsible for the distribution of foreign aid (about $12 billion since 2001) to be used for the construction of roads and housing, for such basic needs as water and electricity, for the widespread distribution of social services, and for providing jobs.

Progress in this direction, however, did not speed up after the parliamentary elections. On the other hand, 2005 saw the beginnings of what appeared to be a destabilizing situation in Afghanistan due to the resurgence of the Taliban. Between 2001 and 2004, the Taliban appeared to have fallen back into their rural strongholds in the south and east near the Pakistani border. But 2005 to 2006 witnessed a

Hamid Karzai, Successor to the Taliban

Genial, engaging, and English-speaking, Hamid Karzai grew up in the Kandahar region of southern Afghanistan. His family, which was ethnically Pashtun, was relatively well off and well educated. Karzai's father had once served as a senator in the Afghan government and Karzai, as a young political organizer, supported the return of the monarchy as a means of unifying the country.

Later, the anti-Soviet jihad, or holy war, of the Taliban drew Hamid Karzai to their side. But an attempt on his life from unknown sources in 1994 sent him into exile in Pakistan, where his father had already sought refuge. As the Taliban became more despotic and destructive, Karzai leveled criticism at them and, in 1999, implored Mullah Omar by letter to modify his rule. Mullah Omar's response came in the form of the assassination—allegedly by Taliban motorcycle gunmen—of Karzai's father in Pakistan.

Karzai, remaining in exile, undertook a campaign to get the United States, as well as European nations, to launch an offensive against the Taliban in Afghanistan. No action was taken, however, until the bombing of the World Trade Center and the Pentagon on September 11, 2001. In November 2001, a month after the American-led anti-Taliban invasion of Afghanistan, Hamid Karzai was chosen at a conference in Bonn, Germany, as the country's interim leader.

Hamid Karzai, who was elected president of Afghanistan in 2004, struggles with the problems of underdevelopment, poverty, corruption, and ongoing Taliban resistance in his war-torn country.

mounting number of attacks on civilians, workers, foreign businesses, policemen, Afghan soldiers, and government officials, resulting in the deaths of hundreds. Also in this period, United States and coalition forces from a variety of European countries stationed in Afghanistan clashed increasingly with the resurgent Taliban and with other insurgents linked to bin Laden's Al Qaeda terror network.

Could the Taliban disrupt or even cause the overthrow of the Karzai government? Much still depends on the amount of support the United States and its allies are able and willing to give to Afghanistan. Since March 2003, when President George W. Bush led the invasion of Iraq, the United States has been preoccupied militarily and financially with the ensuing struggle for stability in that Middle Eastern nation, which some people have termed a quagmire. Meantime, Afghanistan has been called the "forgotten war."

While the strength of the Taliban at the present time is uncertain, there is no question that their attacks have become more lethal and more sophisticated, employing not only suicide bombers but remote-controlled devices. A major source of Taliban funding for their growing campaign of violence is the drug trade.

During Taliban theocratic rule between 1996 and 2001, religious law prohibited farmers from the traditional growing of opium poppies, the lucrative crop that provides both opium and heroin. However, soon after the fall of the Taliban—and despite the efforts of President Karzai—farmers turned from the growing of wheat and other much-needed food crops to poppy cultivation in increasing quantities.

As the supplier of approximately 90 percent of the world's opium, Afghanistan is today a drug trafficker's haven, enriching warlords, corrupt government officials, and the Taliban (with the farmers receiving the smallest share of the profits). No longer do Afghanistan's onetime theocratic rules have a problem with Sharia law prohibiting the cultivation and the use of narcotics.

6
Could Religious Fundamentalism Lead to Future Theocracies?

THE TERM FUNDAMENTALISM first came into use in the early 1900s in the United States when a religious publishing house issued a series of pamphlets defending Protestantism against so-called infidels who were perceived as a threat to the purity of that religion.

Today we use the term to describe fundamentalists of any religion, including Islam, Judaism, and Christianity. A principal belief of fundamentalists is the acceptance of the writings in their holy books—be they the Koran, the Old Testament, or the New Testament—as the word of God. Fundamentalists insist on a back-to-basics adherence to the tenets of their religion. The miraculous-appearing events of its birth and the words of its prophets are never questioned or doubted.

Many religious fundamentalists have been content to practice their beliefs more or less privately or have attempted to influence the society in which they live politically, socially, and culturally without resorting to strong measures or to violence. But others, such as the Saudi Arabian exile Osama bin Laden, have been drawn to extremism in the form of terrorism and mass murder.

After having left his homeland permanently in the early 1990s and been stripped of Saudi Arabian citizenship in 1994, bin Laden never gave up the idea of toppling the Saudi royal family and installing a fundamentalist Islamic government, making Saudi Arabia a powerful oil-rich theocracy. To that end, he bombed not only American military installations in Saudi Arabia in 1995 and 1996, but in May 2003 Al Qaeda attacked three foreign compounds in the Saudi capital of Riyadh. Thirty-five people, many of them Saudis, and including nine Americans, were killed and more than one hundred were wounded.

Similar operations took place in 2004. In December, the U.S. consulate in Jedda, Saudi Arabia, was attacked and five foreign staff members were killed. The same month saw the car bombing of the Saudi Ministry of Information in Riyadh. Kidnappings of foreign camera crews, defense contractors, and engineers took place, one of them resulting in a beheading that was shown on Saudi television.

Although foreigners appeared to be the main target, there was also growing evidence that bin Laden's Al Qaeda operations in Saudi Arabia were directed at destabilizing and weakening the rule of the Saudi royal family. Combatting terrorism within the kingdom became a major operation in the years that followed. By 2006, the Saudi anti-terrorism authorities were able to announce that of Al Qaeda's five major cells consisting of twenty-six "most wanted" members each, all but one member had been killed or captured.

Of so-called secondary Al Qaeda groups in Saudi Arabia, only four individuals were still at large in 2006, an attack in February of that year had been thwarted, and more than 700 other suspected terrorists were under arrest. The cost of anti-terrorism surveillance in 2006—a cost that had been escalating each year since 2004—was $12 billion, including $2 billion to secure the kingdom's all-important oil industry. The threat of religious extremism to the government of Saudi Arabia was nothing new. Its royal family had been having its conflicts since the early 1900s with the fundamentalist Islamic sect known as Wahhabism, of which bin Laden had become an adherent.

THE WAHHABIS AND THE SAUDS

For centuries desert tribes had been leading a nomadic existence in the vast wasteland of Saudi Arabia known as the "Empty Quarter." After the introduction of Islam, the tribal peoples had become mainly Sunni Muslims. The mid–1700s saw the founding of an austere fundamentalist sect led by the Sunni scholar Muhammed bin Abdul Wahhab.

Also an emerging power in the 1700s was Muhammed bin Saud, who ruled a prosperous desert oasis. In 1745, the two formed an alliance for the purpose of conquering the other tribes of the Arabian

Peninsula and forming a kingdom in which the Saud family would serve as temporal, or secular, rulers and the Wahhabis would dictate the religious life of the country.

It was not until the 1920s, however, following the 1918 dissolution of the Ottoman Empire (of which the Arabian Peninsula was a part) that Saudi Arabia gained its independence. Its ruler King Abdul Aziz ibn Saud followed the Muslim polygamous practice of having many wives, and produced forty-five sons (as well as many daughters), five of whom have since served as the nation's ruler.

With the discovery of extensive reserves of oil in the kingdom during the 1930s, the royal family entered into a special relationship with the United States, granting concessions for the technology of drilling and refining its natural resource in return for military protection. In addition, the royal family acquired enormous wealth, enabling its members to live in luxury, travel and study abroad, and employ foreigners with special skills to do jobs for which Saudis were not qualified.

Oil wealth also transformed Saudi Arabia into the welfare state that it is today. Saudi citizens pay no taxes, are given free education through university, and are exempt from menial work, most of which is done by foreign workers from the impoverished Red Sea nation of Yemen.

Politically the kingdom is run much as in the days of tribal governance. All royal decisions are made via consensus in a council meeting known as a *majlis*. Saudi Arabia has no constitution, no parliament, and no political parties. Its male citizens were given their first opportunity to vote in February 2005, but only for one-half of the members of their city councils. The remaining halves and the mayors of cities would continue to be appointed. Women were prohibited from voting.

Throughout Saudi Arabia's development as an independent nation there have been conflicts between the royal family and the strict clergy of Wahhabi Islam. When King Faisal (a son of King Abdul Aziz, who ruled from 1964 to 1975) tried to introduce schools for girls as well as television in the 1960s, he was accused by the religious right of aping the West and was forced to make concessions to the Wahhabis. These included the king's acceptance into the country of exiled fundamentalist scholars from Egypt and the promise that attendance at the schools for girls would not be compulsory and would be limited to basic education and religious subjects.

Wahhabism, the Purest Form of Islam

As Jonathan Randal writes in his book *Osama: The Making of a Terrorist*, "The Wahhabi insist on a stripped-down, just-the-basics, puritanical form of Sunni Islam construed as enforcing the purified faith as practiced by the Prophet Mohammed in the seventh century in their very land."

In adhering strictly to the Koran, Wahhabism prohibits music, dancing, tobacco, and alcohol. It enforces the segregation of the sexes in schools and workplaces and forbids the existence of movie houses in which men and women sit adjacent to one another. Elevators in high-rise buildings must be sex-segregated.

Foreigners working in Saudi Arabia must live in compounds separated from the rest of the population, and no religion other than Islam is authorized to have a place of worship in the nation. In the words of Muhammad as he lay dying, "Let there be no two religions in Arabia."

Women must be veiled when appearing in public, their heads covered and their bodies hidden beneath long, loose garments. They are banned from driving, and those women who have attempted to do so have been arrested by the religious police.

Although women may attend university, the educational emphasis for both men and women throughout their school years is on religion.

The two main professional fields open to women are teaching and medicine. Women students taught by male professors at university receive their education through closed-circuit television.

The traditional punishments for criminal behavior are mutilation for thievery (usually the loss of the right hand), stoning to death for adultery and, for major crimes against the religion or the government, beheading.

Wahhabism has even led to the assassination of a Saudi king. Faisal, the reformist monarch who introduced schools for girls and television during the 1960s, was shot to death in 1975 before an assemblage of the royal family by a dissident nephew who sided with the austere views of the Wahhabi clerics.

King Faisal's attempt to bring television to Saudi Arabia was strongly opposed because of the Muslim ban on the representation of human images. The clergy gave their permission only after Faisal pointed out that the new medium could be used for readings of the Koran. Today even the Wahhabi clergy can do little to prevent TV reception and the Internet in Saudi Arabia, but there are still many restrictions on Saudi citizens that stem from Sharia law and that make for an uneasy alliance between the royal family and the Wahhabi clerics.

COULD WAHHABISM TOPPLE THE MONARCHY?

The Saudi kings appear to have managed so far to balance their secular rule with the demands of the country's fundamentalist religionists. Often they have done so by bowing to the Wahhabi in exchange for permission to import, for example, foreign specialists and technologies to help the nation progress. In return, the royal family's petrodollars (huge sums derived from its oil exports) are used to help fund the spread of fundamentalist Islam to other Muslim countries, as well as the West.

The influence of Wahhabism in Saudi Arabia itself is extensive. Fifteen of the nineteen hijackers in the attack on the United States on September 11, 2001, were Saudis. Jihad is preached constantly through the distrust of outsiders, the hatred of America, infidels, and Jews, and the criticism of the friendship between the royal family and the United States.

The Saudi response to the deaths of some 3,000 Americans on 9/11 included many who denied that it was the work of Osama bin Laden and his Al Qaeda organization but rather an Israeli plot intended to cast blame on Muslims. Fundamentalist Saudis joined the Taliban in Afghanistan to resist the 2001 American invasion that followed 9/11. Saudis also fought with the insurgents in Iraq after the United States invaded that country in 2003.

Fundamentalist Islam in Saudi Arabia has long accused the royal family of corruption and of following Western practices such as drinking and mingling with the opposite sex, especially when visiting or vacationing abroad.

There is also the question of who will succeed the sons of Abdul Aziz ibn Saud as kings. Many of the members of this first royal generation were eighty or older by 2006. Today the Saudi princes who are *their* sons and grandsons live in luxury and are said to number in the thousands. How will the line of succession be decided when the last son of Abdul Aziz dies? Could a fight for the throne lead to civil war, giving the Wahhabi the opportunity to take over the rulership of the country and to convert it into a powerful theocracy on the world stage?

Among ordinary Saudi citizens, there appears to be little drive for reform and liberalization of thought. Generations of schoolchildren are educated in religion to the neglect of the sciences and other branches of the curriculum. Nor did the local elections, instituted for the first time in 2005, show promise of change. Five out of seven councilmen elected were those who were backed by hard-line clerics.

Lastly, what will happen to Saudi Arabia when the oil runs out? Today, the country receives one-quarter of the world's revenues from this valuable resource. But demand is constantly increasing and the supply is finite.

In such a situation, the royal family would be more than likely to lose its grip on power, giving the Wahhabi the long-sought chance to return the land of Muhammad's birth as near as possible to the teachings and principles of the founder of Islam. Meanwhile, the royal family takes few meaningful steps toward reform and continues its uneasy relationship with the religious fundamentalism that rules the kingdom.

THE MUSLIM BROTHERHOOD IN EGYPT

Although a very different Arab nation from Saudi Arabia both historically and politically, Egypt, too, today finds itself threatened by Islamic religious fundamentalists.

Like Saudi Arabia, Egypt was converted to Islam in the 600s CE. But it had already experienced a 4,000-year-old ancient civilization, after which it underwent Greek and Roman rule, and subsequently became Christianized. Even today, 6 to 10 percent of Egypt's population of 76 million are Coptic Christians (whose practices are similar to those of the Eastern Orthodox Church).

Although almost the entire balance of Egyptians—90 to 94 percent—are Sunni Muslims, the government of Egypt has for many decades been secular and does not take direction from its Muslim clergy. Currently the country has a written constitution and a parliament, and is run by a president who is elected for a six-year term.

There has until recently, however, been only one political party in Egypt, the National Democratic Party (NDP), and the country's

Deadly Attacks on Tourists in Egypt

Egypt's ancient treasures—the pyramids, the temples along the Nile, the mummies and works of art in its museums—have lured travelers from around the world for centuries. Between 1992 and 1997, however, British, German, French, Greek, American, Israeli, and other visitors have lost their lives in sporadic bombings of tourist buses, trains, and Nile cruise ships, and at key tourist sites. November 1997 saw sixty-two tourists killed at the city of Luxor on the Nile.

Between 2004 and 2006, the death toll continued to rise as presumably home-grown terrorists, who now appeared to be linked to Al Qaeda, began to attack Egyptian resorts on the Red Sea. In 2004, thirty-four people died in bomb blasts in the Egyptian resort area of Taba, which is frequented by Israeli tourists. On July 23, 2005, eighty-eight people—mainly Egyptian hotel workers—were reportedly killed in a massive bombing in the resort of Sharm el-Sheikh. And a similar attack, which killed twenty-three, took place on April 24, 2006, at Dahab, a scuba-diving site popular with young Europeans and Israelis.

As in previous attacks of this nature, marketplaces, eateries, and tourist bazaars were littered with broken glass, blood, body parts, and articles of clothing blasted from the bodies of the victims. For every person who died in the attack there were, as always, scores of wounded, many with serious injuries.

The Taba Hilton, an Egyptian tourist resort hotel, after it was bombed by fundamentalist Islamic groups in 2004.

constitution has allowed the president to run unopposed and to serve for an unlimited number of terms.

Long-simmering resentment against both Egypt's one-man rule and its secularist government has its roots in the birth in 1928 of a religious organization known as the Muslim Brotherhood. Its founder was a young elementary school teacher named Hassan al-Banna who developed it as a youth organization that advocated a return to the principles of the Koran, and that would eventually have branches in some seventy countries.

The motto of the Muslim Brotherhood indicates its fundamentalist policies. "Allah is our objective. The Prophet is our leader. Qur'an [Koran] is our law. Jihad is our way. Dying in the way of Allah is our highest hope."

The banning of the Brotherhood by the Egyptian government led to the assassination of an Egyptian prime minister in 1948 and subsequently to the death of al-Banna himself by government agents in Cairo in 1949. By this time, the membership of the Muslim Brotherhood in Egypt had grown to half a million.

Another Islamic extremist who lent his ideas to the Brotherhood was Sayyed Qutb, who had made an attempt in 1954 on the life of the Egyptian president Gamal Abdul Nasser, who held office from 1952 to 1970. Qutb felt that violence against nonbelievers was justified, as was any means of seizing political power in Egypt. He had been radicalized by a trip to the United States in 1948, which he described as representative of "a large brothel. One has only to glance at its press, films, fashion shows, beauty contests, ballrooms, wine bars, and broadcasting stations!"

Jailed by Nasser from 1954 to 1964, Qutb made another attempt through the Brotherhood on Nasser's life in 1965, for which he was executed by hanging in 1966. But his influence and the political goals of the Brotherhood lived on and were responsible for the murder of the next president of Egypt, Anwar el-Sadat.

On coming to power in 1970, following Nasser's death due to a heart attack, Sadat attempted to take a more moderate stance toward the Brotherhood. But Sadat's proposal in late 1977 that the former enemy nations of Egypt and Israel open a dialogue for peace led to a death sentence for Sadat. As he sat watching a military parade with members of his government on a reviewing stand in Cairo on October 6, 1981, the peace-minded Sadat was gunned down by men in army uniforms,

Islamic extremists who were the heirs of al-Banna and Qutb.

Sadat's successor, Hosni Mubarak, adopted an emergency law designed to crack down on fundamentalists who believed they had a right to take the lives of those they saw as betraying Islam, and thousands were jailed. But measures against the Brotherhood also bred new and fiercer Islamic radicals. They have included the chief lieutenant and planner of terrorist policy to Osama bin Laden, Ayman al-Zawahiri, an Egyptian jihadist who fled to Afghanistan. Within Egypt, the Muslim Brotherhood and allied groups chose to attack the government of Mubarak by aiming directly at the nation's chief source of foreign income, tourism.

A POLITICAL DILEMMA FOR EGYPT

As the presidential election of the late fall of 2005 approached, the Egyptian president, Hosni Mubarak, prepared to run unopposed, as in the past, for a fifth six-year term. But as one of the few secular governments in the Muslim world (Turkey is the most democratic secular nation in Islam), how could Egypt approach democracy unless its people were given a real choice in national elections? Opposition groups including the Muslim Brotherhood began early in the year to agitate for a change in the nation's constitution to allow for open elections based on a multiparty system.

A popular referendum in May 2005 and an amendment to the constitution in September opened the way to multicandidate elections in November and December. Under the rallying cry "Kefaya" (Enough), a combination of university students, pro-democracy activists, and members of the banned Muslim Brotherhood marched in Cairo and other cities despite confrontations with Mubarak's police.

Mubarak, aware of swelling demand for broader representation, especially by the Muslim Brotherhood, ran on a pro-reform ticket. He was handicapped by Egypt's reputation as a state that is notorious for the practice of torture. He chose the motto "A Free Citizen in a Democratic Country," fearful that a persuasive fundamentalist faction in the election could gain power and eventually turn Egypt into a theocracy.

Mubarak won the 2005 election by a large margin with 88.6 percent of the votes, but through only a small turnout—23 percent of Egypt's thirty-two million registered voters. The limited voting in the presidential election was very likely an indication of the many faults

In 2005, President Hosni Mubarak of Egypt was elected to his fifth six-year term, in spite of having opened the voting to opposition groups for the first time.

that members of the Muslim Brotherhood, especially, find with the present government. In 2006, Egypt was plagued with corruption, tax evasion, a population explosion that has resulted in a large unemployed youth population, and a lack of government-provided social services.

The Muslim Brotherhood, on the other hand, has engaged the Egyptian public with its health, education, and welfare programs. Even though it could not run candidates on a party basis, it was able to win 20 percent of the seats in Egypt's 454-member parliament in the 2005 elections.

The dilemma for Egypt is as follows: Will the attempt to democratize a state that has been criticized for its harsh treatment of its fundamentalist dissidents result in the radical Islamic takeover of a formerly secular government?

THE RELIGIOUS RIGHT IN ISRAEL

Islam is not the only source of fundamentalist extremism threatening to overturn secular governments and replace them with theocratic rule. Rumblings from the religious right are also heard in the democratic nation of the State of Israel, where Jewish fundamentalism has existed for decades and appears to be growing stronger due to a number of factors.

These include opposition to a peaceful solution to the Palestinian problem through the creation of a separate Palestinian state within Israel, as well as opposition to the withdrawal of Jewish settlements built on Palestinian land. A vivid example of settler resistance was seen in the violent incidents that took place in 2005 on the occasion of the government-mandated withdrawal of Jewish settlements from the Gaza Strip on Israel's western coast.

As a homeland for Jews of all political and religious viewpoints, Israel has long had a strong religious hierarchy that has been given authority over such matters as marriage, divorce, adoption, and burial not only among Orthodox Jews but for all of Israel's citizens. In other words, Jews who do not conform to the rules of Orthodox Judaism (as opposed to the somewhat looser Conservative and Reform versions of the faith, as well as secularism) may not be married in Israel, where there are only religious but no civil marriage laws.

As a result, non-Orthodox Israelis must marry abroad. Many go to the Mediterranean island of Cyprus, others to Italy, and some to the United States and even the Dominican Republic, where civil ceremonies

Militant Jewish settlers fight against the Israeli government's 2005 order to evacuate the Gaza Strip, rightfully considered to be Palestinian territory.

can be obtained. Similar problems exist with regard to divorce, and adoptions are not sanctioned unless both prospective parents are Orthodox Jews, and the child is of Jewish birth. Many burial grounds, too, are closed to the non-Orthodox.

As Israel does not have a written constitution or a bill of rights, the Israeli Parliament (known as the Knesset) is responsible for all legislation. The Israeli High Court (the judicial equivalent of the United States Supreme Court) has often done battle with the rabbinical hierarchy of the religious right in an attempt to broaden the legal status of non-Orthodox Jews in ceremonial lifecycle events that are part of the Jewish faith. In response, the religious right has labeled the court's chief justice an enemy of the Jews.

It is estimated that today 20 to 25 percent of Israel's population are hard-core rightists who identify strongly with Jewish fundamentalism. What would a Jewish theocratic State of Israel be like?

In the words of David Hirst, writing in *The Nation* magazine in February 2004, "the Jewish Kingdom that arose . . . would elevate a stern and wrathful God's sovereignty over any new-fangled heathen concepts such as the people's will, civil liberties, or human rights. It would be governed by the *Halacha*, or Jewish religious law, of which the rabbis would be the sole interpreters."

Halacha (which is similar in origin and application to Sharia, or Koranic law, among fundamentalist Muslims) demands the segregation of men and women in public, female covering of the hair and most of the body, and severe punishments such as stoning women to death for adultery. Religious laws banning driving and other activities that violate the Sabbath are already in effect in Orthodox quarters of Jerusalem, and the entire city is without public transportation from Friday evening to Saturday evening. Under theocratic rule such prohibitions with regard to the Sabbath would no doubt be extended to all of Israel.

Various Jewish fundamentalist groups have come together to form the religious right in Israel. While they may disagree on some matters, all appear to be in agreement regarding the need for a Jewish Kingdom that will usher in the long-awaited coming of the Messiah. Leader and deliverer of the Jewish people, the Messiah will rebuild the Temple (last destroyed in 70 CE by the Roman legions).

A second and perhaps even stronger meeting of the minds among Israeli rightists stems from the settler movement, comprising those

Jews who have lived for years in the disputed territories of Gaza and the West Bank of Israel, and who have numbered some 400,000 scattered throughout about two hundred settlements.

The basic belief of the militant settler movement has been that God willed all of the land of the current State of Israel to the Jewish people, and that it is their birthright to drive off any Palestinians and to occupy it fully. In addition, as sanctioned by Orthodox rabbis in both Israel and abroad, the settlers were empowered to take vengeance on any Jew who attempted to imperil the life or property of another Jew by attempting to secure peace through the division of the land between Palestinians and Jews.

It was this indictment based on fundamentalist law that led to the murder of an Israeli prime minister by a fanatic young Israeli allied with the settler movement.

IS THERE AN ISRAELI THREAT FROM WITHIN?

Fiercest among the many splinter groups that have come together to make war on a secular and democratic Israeli state are those that have been inspired by the Brooklyn-born rabbi Meir Kahane. Kahane, who immigrated to Israel, preached the expulsion of all Arabs and was elected to the Israeli parliament. So violent was his religious zealotry that his movement, known as Kach, was eventually outlawed in Israel. Kahane met his death in 1990 in New York at the hands of an Arab assassin.

The Kahanist ideology lives on among many extremist settlers. Probably the most notorious are the recently emerged "hilltop people," also known as the "hilltop youth" because most are teenagers and young adults, the offspring of settlers who are determined to hold onto their land regardless of any government edicts to move them.

To stake out additional territory, the hilltop youth (who are estimated to number several thousand) build frontier outposts and even crude synagogues atop hills on Israel's West Bank. As a result, they have frequent clashes with Israel's police and military forces.

Even more serious have been the youths' attacks on the Palestinians who legally occupy nearby lands. These attacks range from cutting down centuries-old Palestinian olive groves to random shootings of Arabs seen as "trespassing" on Jewish land.

An attempt in 2002 by the hilltop youth to murder Palestinian schoolgirls in East Jerusalem by planting a bomb-laden trailer beside

The Militant Settlers and the Murder of Yitzhak Rabin

The world was shocked on November 4, 1995, when Yitzak Rabin, the Israeli prime minister who had sought to make peace with the Palestinians by offering them limited self-rule in both Gaza and part of the West Bank, was assassinated at a public gathering in Israel. Only one year earlier, in 1994, Rabin had been awarded the Nobel Peace Prize.

Rabin's murderer was not a Palestinian hostile to the fact that the peace plan, drawn up two years earlier, did not go far enough. He was an Israeli extremist, Yigal Amir, who opposed offering any land to the Palestinians that might threaten the Jewish settlers on the West Bank.

Not unlike another peace-seeker, Anwar el-Sadat (assassinated by members of the extremist Muslim Brotherhood in 1981), a national leader met his death at the hands of a religious fundamentalist of his own nationality.

Even though some of the Jewish settlements on the West Bank had originally been founded illegally, the Orthodox rabbis who were the leaders of the religious right ordered the settlers to disobey military commands to evacuate the occupied lands. From the early 1990s on, they branded Prime Minister Rabin a "traitor" and made strong suggestions as to his fate. In effect, fundamentalist Judaism was offering a license to kill to any extremist who agreed with the biblical decree that only Jews were destined to live on Israeli land.

their school was intercepted by the police. The young men who made up the Jewish terror cell were apprehended and given prison terms of twelve to fifteen years. But militant settlers and religious rightists viewed their punishment as martyrdom, and an organized Jewish underground has only been strengthened as a result.

Many other problems exist for the Israeli government. In January 2006, the powerful Israeli prime minister Ariel Sharon, who was engaged in reshaping the future of the state, collapsed and fell into a deep, irreversible coma. And in that same month the Palestinian people held parliamentary elections that gave legislative control to the most militant of its political parties, Hamas. Leadership for Israel and accommodation with the Palestinians became more pressing issues than ever before.

It is the long-term goal of Jewish fundamentalism to destroy Israeli democracy and to install a theocratic kingdom based on the literal interpretation of the Bible. Only when all Arabs are driven from the land and it is occupied solely by its Jewish inheritors can God reveal himself and send the Messiah to earth. And with "Kahane lives on!" continuing as a major slogan of the militant Israeli right, one cannot help wondering if Israel may be facing war, not over the long-disputed Palestinian problem, but with itself.

THE DANGEROUS BLURRING OF CHURCH AND STATE IN THE UNITED STATES

The swell of religious fundamentalism in a number of nations around the world today appears to be a threat to their stability, regardless of their political systems. An endangered nation may be a monarchy, such as Saudi Arabia, a republic with traditional one-man rule, such as Egypt, or even a democracy such as Israel.

Other world democracies also find themselves needing to be constantly vigilant concerning the encroachment of religion into government affairs and civil life, lest matters of church and state become blurred.

Many people justifiably view the United States as a purely secular nation in which the two are separate and distinct. One need only examine the Constitution and the Bill of Rights (the first ten amendments) to ascertain that it was not the intention of the founders of 1789 to introduce religion into government.

"We the People of the United States . . . do ordain and establish this Constitution," reads the well-known Preamble. It does *not* read, "Recognizing Almighty God as the source of all authority and power in civil government, and acknowledging the Lord Jesus Christ as the Governor among the nations . . . in order to constitute a Christian government . . ."

The foregoing—a suggested rewording of the Preamble—was actually presented to President Abraham Lincoln in 1864 by a Christian fundamentalist group that felt religion should enter into the Constitution, perhaps to give the North some spiritual advantage over the South in the Civil War.

Lincoln rejected the petition of the Protestant fundamentalists to Christianize the Constitution. But it was in that time of bitter fighting that Congress agreed to add the phrase "In God We Trust" to American coins, which remains with us today. "In God We Trust" was absent from paper currency well into the 1900s. And the words "under God" were added to the Pledge of Allegiance in 1954, as a response to the "godless" Soviet Union, which was regarded as a national threat.

Religion, where it is mentioned in the Constitution, is swept away as a qualification for public office holders: "no religious Test shall ever be required" (Article VI, Section 3). And the First Amendment, ratified in 1791, declares that "Congress shall make no law respecting an establishment of religion, or prohibiting the free exercise thereof . . ."

Yet, during the more than two centuries since the Constitution was written, there have been cycles during which secularism in government and in public life has been markedly challenged by the religious right. One of these cycles appears to be the post–9/11 era. Perhaps this is so because an overwhelmingly Christian United States perceives itself to be threatened by Muslim fundamentalism.

On September 13, 2001, two days after the bombing of the World Trade Center and the Pentagon by the Islamist terrorist organization Al Qaeda, the Reverend Jerry Falwell voiced the following opinion. Falwell, a popular televangelist and founder of the religious rightist Moral Majority, blamed "the pagans, and the abortionists, and the feminists, and the gays and the lesbians . . . who have tried to secularize America" for having made "God mad."

As a result of "throwing God out successfully with the help of the federal court system, throwing God out of the public square, out of the schools," Falwell stated, Americans [who were abiding by the secularist laws of the land] were responsible for the attack. "I point the finger in their face," Falwell concluded, "and say: 'You helped this happen.'"

Examples of clashes between religious expression and the laws of a non-theocratic nation that question the intrusion of faith-based issues into public life abound. They range from whether Christmas symbols should appear in the public squares of cities and towns across America to the more serious matter of whether prayer and even the teaching of religion should be permitted in public schools.

Should courthouses in the United States be permitted to display copies of the Ten Commandments? Should a justice of the United States Supreme Court (Justice Antonin Scalia) state—in contradiction of the premises of the U.S. Constitution—that the Ten Commandments are "a symbol of the fact that government derives its authority from God?"

Aren't we inching, albeit very slowly, in the direction of theocratic principles when the policies of the president of the United States are based on his personal relationship with God (derived in part from the president's earlier experience with alcoholism)? Should President George W. Bush, elected in 2000 and reelected in 2004, appoint judges to federal courts on the basis of their religious conservatism? Should his personal religious view (that life begins at conception even under laboratory conditions) result in his severely limiting national funding for stem-cell research (which holds the scientific promise of saving human lives)?

Above all, should fundamentalist Protestants, right-wing Catholics, and other extreme Christian groups take an active stand toward having the United States declared a "Christian nation," when its founders made not a single reference to God in its Constitution and guaranteed freedom of religion as well as freedom *from* religion to all its people?

In 1960, John F. Kennedy, only the second Roman Catholic in history to run for president of the United States on a major-party ticket, felt that it was necessary for him to explain "not what kind of church I believe in . . . but what kind of America I believe in."

Speaking in Houston, Texas to an audience of largely Protestant ministers on September 12, Kennedy said the following. "I believe in an America where the separation of church and state is absolute—where no Catholic prelate would tell the President (should he be a Catholic) how to act and no Protestant minister would tell his parishioners for whom to vote." Kennedy also warned against government support via public funds of religious institutions and against political preferences based on religious principles.

Is the wall between church and state in the United States today crumbling? Has the fear and loathing engendered by Muslim fundamentalist acts of terrorism led to a frenzied reaction on the part of right-wing Americans of faith?

Or can we look forward to a return to the principles of the world's first secular government, as drawn up by the founders? In that government, every individual has the freedom to engage in any religion or in none, without prejudice. Even more important—if even the slightest hints of theocracy are to be totally absent from the political scene—the leaders of that government must base their policies not on faith but on carefully considered fact.

Theocracy and Other Governments

THEOCRACY	COMMUNISM	SOCIALISM
Often only one legal political party	Only one legal political party (Communist Party)	Multiple legal political parties; limited electoral freedom
Limited or no electoral freedom; rule by a single individual or small group	No free elections; rule by a single individual or small group	Rule by people through elections, although individual or small group may dominate politics
Opposition and dissent are limited or forbidden	Opposition and dissent are limited or forbidden	Opposition and dissent may be limited
Limited property rights	No private property	Limited property rights
Government may have a significant role in economy	State-controlled economy	Government has significant role in economy
Unemployment determined by free market and government policy	Officially no unemployment	Unemployment determined by combination of the free market and government policy
Religious worship limited to the state religion	No freedom of religion; limited or no civil liberties or civil rights	May have religious freedom; civil liberties and civil rights may be curtailed by government, especially economic rights
Limited or no civil liberties or civil rights; social welfare programs are limited	Widespread social welfare programs (such as free education and health care)	Widespread social welfare programs (such as free education, health care, and housing)

DEMOCRACY	DICTATORSHIP	MONARCHY*
Multiple legal political parties	Often only one legal political party	May have no legal political parties, or only one
Free rule by the people through elections	Limited or no electoral freedom	Limited or no electoral freedom; rule by a single individual; monarchy may be hereditary or elective
Opposition and dissent are accepted and may be encouraged	Rule by a single individual; opposition and dissents are limited or forbidden	Opposition and dissent may be limited or forbidden
Private property protected by law and constitution	Limited property rights	Limited property rights, usually inherited; monarch may claim ownership of entire kingdom
Economy determined by free market	Government may have significant role in economy	Government may have significant role in economy
Unemployment determined mainly by the free market	Unemployment determined by combination of the free market and government policy	Monarch may determine how people are to be employed; forced labor may be required
Freedom of religion	Some religious freedom, if it does not threaten the regime	Religious freedom may be allowed if it does not threaten the regime—or not, depending on ruler
Widespread and comprehensive civil liberties and civil rights; some social welfare	Limited or no civil liberties and civil rights; social welfare programs are limited	Social welfare programs may be limited

*Monarchy here refers to absolute monarchy, the traditional form of monarchy known in many earlier kingdoms but rare today; modern constitutional monarchies are monarchies in name only and are typically governed as democratic or Socialist republics.

Timeline

632
Muhammad, founder and prophet of Islam, born in Mecca, Arabia, in about 570 CE, dies leaving no designated successor.

680
Muhammad's grandson Hussein, son of his daughter and son-in-law Ali, is killed at the battle of Karbala in Iraq by a Muslim army that opposed Ali as the true successor to Muhammad. Thus a split in the religion divides Shia Muslims (partisans of Ali) from Sunni Muslims (partisans of the caliphs that were appointed to succeed Muhammad).

1501
Under an Iranian dynasty known as the Safavids, Shia Islam becomes the state religion of Iran.

1925
Reza Shah Pahlavi becomes ruler of the Iranian monarchy and tries to modernize the nation and to institute reforms that include the liberation of women from the restrictions of Islamic law.

1941
Reza Shah abdicates and the throne goes to his son Mohammed Reza Shah Pahlavi. He combines dictatorial powers with attempts at pro-Western modernization and is forced to abdicate in 1979 in the face of an Islamic revolution led by the fundamentalist Islamic cleric Ayatollah Ruhollah Khomeini.

1979
Khomeini and the Shia religious extremists, supported by a large student movement, establish a theocratic government and take fifty-two American hostages, who are held captive for 444 days.

1980

The Iran-Iraq War breaks out and lasts until 1988, taking close to a million lives.

1989

On February 14 Khomeini issues a *fatwa* condemning the Indian-British writer Salman Rushdie to death for his book *The Satanic Verses* because it is irreverent to Islam. On June 3, the Ayatollah Khomeini dies of a heart attack and is succeeded as Supreme Leader by Ayatollah Ali Khamenei.

1997

Mohammed Khatami is elected president of Iran with hope on the part of moderates, intellectuals, and the new youth generation that he will institute some reforms. But the hard-line religious leaders who oversee the presidency prevent any significant liberalization during his two terms in office.

2005

Iran is accused by the United States and other nations of enriching uranium for the purpose of building nuclear weapons. Iran's adherence to the Nuclear Nonproliferation Treaty of the United Nations Security Council is doubtful, as it elects as its new president a hard-line conservative, Mahmoud Ahmadinejad, who appears determined to maintain a theocratic regime that is independent of world opinion.

2006

Ahmadinejad continues Iran's enrichment of uranium for questionable purposes in defiance of global pressure. His control of a large oil supply, of international terrorist groups, and of Shiite influence in the Iraq war make him a formidable threat.

Timeline

THE ANCIENT WORLD: AN EGYPTIAN THEOCRACY

5000 BCE
Agriculture begins to flourish on the banks of Egypt's Nile River.

3100 BCE
Northern and southern Egypt are unified under one ruler who is deemed to be divine and is supported by a vast priesthood to serve the nation's many gods.

2649–2150 BCE
During this period, known as the Old Kingdom, the theocratic rulers of ancient Egypt build the pyramids that serve as their burial sites. The royal tombs are equipped with necessities and luxuries for the afterlife, throughout which the mummified kings will intercede with the gods on behalf of their people.

1479–1458 BCE
Queen Hatshepsut is Egypt's only woman of her era to rule as sole monarch—and she does so for twenty years. However, unlike most theocratic societies, women of all classes in ancient Egypt have important rights, including the ownership of property and employment opportunities outside the home.

1349–1336 BCE
The pharaoh Akhenaten tries to introduce monotheism, discarding Egypt's many gods and decreeing the worship of a single god, the Aten or sun disk. His idea fails and, on his death, Egypt reverts to its former beliefs.

1336–1327 BCE
The nine-year-old boy king Tutankhamen succeeds Akhenaten and becomes famous chiefly for the discovery, in 1922, of his small but magnificent rock-cut tomb in the Valley of the Kings.

1279–1213 BCE
Ramses II is the last of the powerful pharaohs who sought to expand the empire, erecting monuments to his achievements throughout the land.

332–323 BCE
Alexander the Great conquers Egypt.

51–30 BCE
The rule of the Greek queen Cleopatra VII is followed by the Roman takeover. Both Greeks and Romans in Egypt adopt the practice of mummification and the Egyptian belief in the divine nature of their rulers and the existence of the afterlife.

600s CE
Islam is introduced to Egypt, which becomes a primarily Muslim nation.

Timeline

MESOAMERICAN THEOCRACIES: THE MAYA AND THE AZTECS

5000 BCE
The cultivation of the corn plant in Mesoamerica probably begins.

1000–300 BCE
Settled village life in the highlands, rain forests, and tropical lowlands of Central America leads to the belief in an array of gods responsible for natural phenomena and hence human survival.

250–900 CE
This is the Classic Period of Maya civilization during which city-states numbering 20,000 to 60,000 people are ruled by divine kings whose religious dictates must be followed. Self-mutilation is practiced for the purpose of bloodletting, and human sacrifices are made to the gods. At the same time, Maya civilization makes outstanding advances in mathematics, writing, the sciences, and the arts.

1325–1521
The Aztecs of Central Mexico establish an empire of 300,000 that includes neighboring peoples from whom they exact tribute and human sacrifice victims. Their theocratic rulers ordain almost constant warfare and a rigid class system. Yet, like the Maya, they build magnificent pyramids and palaces and are advanced in the sciences and the arts.

1502
Spanish explorers make their first contact with the Maya off the coast of Honduras.

1519
A Spanish invasion force under Hernán Cortés reaches Mexico. In 1521 Cortés conquers the Aztec empire and introduces the Catholic faith to Mesoamerica.

1542
The subjugation of the Maya by Spain and their conversion to Catholicism enters its final phase.

Timeline

A CHRISTIAN THEOCRACY: MORMONS IN THE YOUNG UNITED STATES

1805
Joseph Smith is born on December 23 in Vermont.

1820
Joseph, age fourteen and living in upper New York State, has his first vision of God and Jesus.

1823
The angel Moroni announces the existence of the golden plates in the hill Cumorah.

1827
Joseph is given the plates to translate. He marries Emma Hale.

1830
The golden plates yield the Book of Mormon and the Mormon religion is born.

1831
The Mormons move their community from New York State to Kirtland, Ohio, and also plan a new Holy Land site on the Missouri frontier.

1833
Violence erupts between the theocratically governed Mormons and non–Mormon Missouri settlers.

1838
The Haun's Mill Massacre drives 8,000 Mormons from Missouri to Nauvoo, Illinois, and lands Joseph Smith in a Missouri jail.

1841
Joseph Smith has a revelation that the dead may be baptized into the Mormon faith by proxy.

1843
It is divinely revealed to Joseph Smith that the Mormons should practice polygamy or "plural marriage."

1844
Joseph Smith prepares to run for United States president on the non-democratic principles he has used to govern the Mormon communities. He smashes the press of a newspaper denouncing polygamy. He is jailed in Carthage, Illinois, to await trial and is murdered there by an angry mob on June 27.

1846
Brigham Young, who has succeeded Joseph Smith, starts the Mormon exodus to the western wilderness that becomes the Utah Territory in 1850. Brigham Young endorses polygamy and threatens dissidents with damnation.

1857
Under Brigham Young as governor, the Mormons come into sharp conflict with the federal government as a result of the Mormon-inflicted Mountain Meadows Massacre.

1877
Brigham Young dies.

1890
The Mormon church imposes an official ban on polygamy in order to gain statehood for Utah (granted in 1896), but Mormon fundamentalists continue the practice into the present.

Timeline

A TALIBAN THEOCRACY: AFGHANISTAN IN THE 1990S

1919
Afghanistan becomes an independent monarchy under the reform-minded king Amanullah Khan, who is overthrown and exiled in 1929.

1933
King Zahir Shah (son of Nadir Khan, who ruled from 1929 to 1933, when he was assassinated) takes the throne. Zahir Shah rules as a pro-reformist until 1973, when he is overthrown by his cousin Mohammed Daoud and is exiled.

1973
Daoud takes control with the title of president, accepting aid from both the United States and the Soviet Union, until he is executed by Soviet-backed Afghan leftists in 1978.

1979
Soviet invaders backed by Afghan communists take over the government. They are opposed by the mujahedeen guerrillas, who are aided by the United States, and finally withdraw in 1989, due to both anti–Soviet fighting and the imminent collapse of the Soviet Union.

1989
The interim government of the mujahedeen is weakened by internal squabbling and starts to dissolve by the early 1990s.

1994
The Taliban, a fundamentalist Muslim army from the Pashtun south of Afghanistan, under the leadership of Mullah Mohammed Omar, take the city of Kandahar.

1996
The Taliban capture Kabul, the capital, and extend their theocratic rule over most of Afghanistan. Osama bin Laden, the Saudi Arabian

Muslim fundamentalist and anti-American terrorist, moves his base of operations to Afghanistan.

2001
On September 11, bin Laden's Al Qaeda terrorist organization launches a massive attack on the United States, killing some 3,000 Americans. On October 7, U.S. and international troops invade Afghanistan, working with the Northern Alliance in an effort to oust the Taliban.

2002
Hamid Karzai is elected president of Afghanistan by a traditional grand council known as a *loya jirga.*

2004
In a national election, in which 8 to 10 million out of Afghanistan's population of 28 million cast their votes, Karzai is elected to a five-year term as president.

2005
A national election to vote for members of parliament takes place in September. However, pockets of Taliban resistance remain in Afghanistan, and Afghans are still in need of basic necessities such as water, roads, electricity, and housing.

2006
Taliban terrorist activity is on the rise, challenging Afghan citizens and U.S. and other foreign troops, causing deaths in the hundreds. Funding for the Taliban comes from the illegal opium poppy trade. Osama bin Laden and Mullah Omar are still at large.

Notes

Foreword
p. 13, "I remember standing in a window . . .": Robert D. McFadden, et al., *No Hiding Place*, p. 4.

Chapter 1
p. 25, "This is a new administration.": Mehran Kamrava, *The Political History of Modern Iran*, p. 68.

p. 25, "I do not remember . . .": Azar Nafisi, *Reading Lolita in Tehran*, p. 104.

p. 25, "slogans that read . . .": Ibid.

p. 26, "People were bused . . .": Ibid., p. 105.

p. 26, "carrying out the people's verdict.": Robert D. McFadden, et al., *No Hiding Place*, p. 255.

p. 28, "Criminals should not be tried.": Nafisi, *Reading Lolita in Tehran*, p. 96.

p. 28, Name: Omid Gharib: Ibid., pp. 96–97.

p. 29, "Women are important . . . only . . .": Oriana Fallaci, *Interview with History*, NY: Liveright, 1976, pp. 271–272.

p. 30, VEILING IS . . . : Nafisi, *Reading Lolita in Tehran*, p. 27.

p. 31, dress . . . as a source of "social corruption": http://www.feminist.org/news/newsbyte/uswirestory (accessed July 26, 2004).

p. 31, "immoral fiction": Azar Nafisi, *Reading Lolita in Tehran*, p. 136.

p. 32, "I moved too rapidly . . .": Mohammad Reza Pahlavi, *Answer to History*, NY: Stein & Day, 1980, p. 116.

p. 36, "drinking the cup of poison": Ibid., p. 238.

p. 38, "Ebadi represents Reformed Islam . . .": http://nobelprize.org/peace/laureate/2003/ebadi-bio.html (accessed September 22, 2004).

p. 40, "The future of this country . . .": *PBS Wide Angle*: "Red Lines and Deadlines–June 2004."

p. 41, "A nuclear program is our irrefutable right": Michael Slackman, "In Iran, Dissenting Voices Rise on Its Leaders' Nuclear Strategy," *New York Times*, March 15, 2006.

Chapter 3

p. 64, "In an eyewitness account": Diego de Landa. *Relacion de las Cosas de Yucatán (Account of the Affairs of Yucatan)*, NY: Kraus Reprint Corp., 1966.

p. 65, "They (the ancestors) said . . .": Richard F. Townsend, *The Aztecs*, p. 117.

Chapter 4

p. 75, "In 303 Diocletian ordered . . .": John C. Dwyer, *Church History*, p. 92.

p. 83, "He was big, powerful . . .": Fawn M. Brodie, *No Man Knows My History*, p. 32.

p. 84, "A viler imposition . . .": Ibid., p. 82.

p. 84, "He believed in the good life . . .": Fawn M. Brodie, *No Man Knows My History*, pp. 294–295.

p. 84, "The enemy in the secret chambers . . .": Joseph Smith, *History of the Church of Jesus Christ of Latter-day Saints*. Ed. B. H. Roberts, 7 vols. Salt Lake City, UT: Church of Jesus Christ of Latter-day Saints, 1932–1951.

p. 84, "endowed with power from on high . . .": Ibid.

p. 86, "martyr-mongers": Fawn M. Brodie, *No Man Knows My History*, p. 259.

p. 87, "Nauvoo's charter . . .": Richard N. Ostling and Joan K. Ostling, *Mormon America*, p. 7.

p. 87, "civic and religious power overlapped . . .": Ibid.

p. 87, "King, Priest and Ruler . . .": Ibid., p. 13.

p. 88, "Monogamy seemed to him . . .": Fawn M. Brodie, *No Man Knows My History*, p. 297.

p. 89, "There is not a nation . . .": Ibid., p. 364.

p. 89, "We do not believe . . .": Ibid., p. 375.

pp. 93–94, "As one might expect of any change . . .": Richard N. Ostling and Joan K. Ostling, *Mormon America*, p. 72.

p. 96, "If any of you will deny . . .": Jon Krakauer, *Under the Banner of Heaven,* p. 203.

Chapter 5
p. 101, "simple band of dedicated youths . . .": quoted in Steve Coll, *Ghost Wars,* p. 289 (from *Time,* October 1, 2001).
p. 101, "The Taliban will fight . . .": quoted in Steve Coll, *Ghost Wars,* p. 289, (from *Associated Press,* September 20, 2001).
p. 105, "arrogance and haughtiness": Peter L. Bergen, *Holy War, Inc.: Inside the Secret World of Osama bin Laden,* NY: Free Press, 2001, p. 19.

Chapter 6
p. 116, "The Wahhabi insist on a stripped-down . . .": Jonathan Randal, *Osama,* p. 49.
p. 122, "Allah is our Objective.":
en.wikipedia.org/wiki/Muslim_Brotherhood
(accessed April 15, 2005).
p. 122, "a large brothel . . .": Steve Coll, *Ghost Wars,* pp. 112–113.
p. 127, "the Jewish Kingdom that arose . . .": David Hirst, "Pursuing the Millenium: Jewish Fundamentalism in Israel," *The Nation,* February 2004.
p. 128, "attempt . . . by . . . hilltop youth to murder Palestinian schoolgirls": *PBS Frontline,* "Israel's Next War," April 2005.
p. 131, "Recognizing Almighty God . . .": Susan Jacoby, *Free Thinkers: A History of American Secularism,* NY: Henry Holt, 2004.
p. 131, "the pagans, and the abortionists . . .": quoted in Bruce Lincoln, *Holy Terrors,* p. 36: Transcript of Pat Robertson's interview with Jerry Falwell broadcast on the *700 Club,* September 13, 2001, http://www.pfaw.org/issues/right/Robertson_Falwell, html
p. 132, "what kind of America I believe in." Hendrik Hertzberg, "New-Time Religion," *The New Yorker,* June 7, 2004, p. 34.

Further Information

BOOKS

Krakauer, Jon. *Under the Banner of Heaven: A Story of Violent Faith.* New York: Doubleday, 2003.

Nafisi, Azar. *Reading Lolita in Tehran: A Memoir in Books.* New York: Random House, 2003.

Perl, Lila. *The Ancient Maya.* Danbury, CT: Franklin Watts/Scholastic, 2005.

Seierstad, Anse. *The Bookseller of Kabul.* Boston, MA: Little, Brown, 2003.

Townsend, Richard F. *The Aztecs.* New York: Thames & Hudson, Revised Edition, 2000.

Williams, Mary E., ed. *The Middle East: Opposing Viewpoints.* San Diego, CA: Greenhaven Press, 2000.

WEB SITES

CQ Press: Theocracy
http://www.cqpress.com/context/articles/epr_theo.html

On the Brink of Theocracy
http://www.commondreams.org/views 05/0506-31.htm

Theocracy Watch
http://www.theocracywatch.org—31k

Word IQ: Theocracy
http://www.wordiq.com/definition/Theocracy

Bibliography

Almond, Gabriel A., R. Scott Appleby, and Emmanuel Sivan. *Strong Religion: The Rise of Fundamentalism around the World.* Chicago, IL: University of Chicago Press, 2003.

Area Handbook Series. *Iran: A Country Study.* Washington, DC: U.S. Government Printing Office, 4th ed., 1989.

Bergen, Peter L. *Holy War, Inc.: Inside the Secret World of Osama bin Laden.* New York: Free Press, 2001.

Brodie, Fawn M. *No Man Knows My History: The Life of Joseph Smith.* New York: Vintage, 2nd ed., 1971.

Cantor, Norman F. *Antiquity: The Civilization of the Ancient World.* New York: HarperCollins, 2003.

Coe, Michael D. *The Maya.* New York: Thames & Hudson, 6th ed., 1999.

Coll, Steve. *Ghost Wars: The Secret History of the CIA, Afghanistan, and bin Laden, from the Soviet Invasion to September 10, 2001.* New York: The Penguin Press, 2004.

Dwyer, John C. *Church History: Twenty Centuries of Catholic Christianity.* Mahwah, NJ: Paulist Press, 1998.

Fallaci, Oriana. *Interview with History.* New York: Liveright, 1976.

Jacoby, Susan. *Freethinkers: A History of American Secularism.* New York: Henry Holt, 2004.

Kamrava, Mehran. *The Political History of Modern Iran: From Tribalism to Theocracy.* Westport: CT: Praeger, 1992.

Krakauer, Jon. *Under the Banner of Heaven: A Story of Violent Faith.* New York: Doubleday, 2003.

Landa, Diego de. *Relación de las Cosas de Yucatán (Account of the Affairs of Yucatan).* New York: Kraus Reprint Corp., 1966.

Lincoln, Bruce. *Holy Terrors: Thinking About Religion after September 11.* Chicago: University of Chicago Press, 2003.

Marsden, Peter. *The Taliban: War, Religion, and the New Order in Afghanistan.* London, England: Zed Books, Ltd., 1998.

McFadden, Robert D., Joseph B. Treaster, and Maurice Carroll. *No Hiding Place: The New York Times Inside Report on the Hostage Crisis.* New York: Times Books, 1981.

Nafisi, Azar. *Reading Lolita in Tehran: A Memoir in Books.* New York: Random House, 2003.

Ostling, Richard N., and Joan K. Ostling. *Mormon America: The Power and the Promise.* New York: HarperCollins, 1999.

Pahlavi, Mohammad Reza. *Answer to History.* New York: Stein & Day, 1980.

Phillips, Kevin. *American Theocracy: The Peril and Politics of Radical Religion, Oil, and Borrowed Money in the 21st Century.* New York: Viking, 2006.

Randal, Jonathan. *Osama: The Making of a Terrorist.* New York: Knopf, 2004.

Seierstad, Anse. *The Bookseller of Kabul.* Boston: Little, Brown, 2003.

Shaw, Ian, ed. *The Oxford History of Ancient Egypt.* New York: Oxford University Press, 2000.

Smith, Joseph. *History of the Church of Jesus Christ of Latter-day Saints.* Ed. B. H. Roberts. 7 vols. Salt Lake City, UT: Church of Jesus Christ of Latter-day Saints, 1932–1951.

Townsend, Richard F. *The Aztecs.* New York: Thames & Hudson, revised edition, 2000.

Williams, Mary E. *The Middle East: Opposing Viewpoints.* San Diego, CA: Greenhaven Press, 2000.

Wright, Lawrence. "Lives of the Saints," *The New Yorker,* January 28, 2002.

Zophy, Jonathan W. *A Short History of Renaissance and Reformation Europe: Dances over Fire and Water.* Upper Saddle River, NJ: Prentice-Hall, 3rd ed., 2003.

Index

Page numbers in **boldface** are illustrations, maps, or charts.

Index ▌▌▌▌▌▌

About the Author

LILA PERL has published more than sixty books for young people and adults, including fiction and nonfiction. Her nonfiction writings have been mainly in the fields of social history, family memoir, and biography. She has traveled extensively to do cultural and background studies of seven African countries, as well as China, Puerto Rico, Guatemala, and Mexico. She has written on subjects as diverse as foods and food customs, genealogy, Egyptian mummies, Latino popular culture, and the Holocaust.

Two of her books have been honored with American Library Association Notable awards: *Red-Flannel Hash and Shoo-Fly Pie* and *Four Perfect Pebbles*. Ten titles have been selected as Notable Children's Trade Books in the Field of Social Studies. Lila Perl has also received a Boston Globe Horn Book award, a Sidney Taylor Committee award, and a Young Adults' Choice award from the International Reading Association. The New York Public Library has cited her work among Best Books for the Teen Age. Her most recent book for Marshall Cavendish Benchmark was *Cloning*, in our Open for Debate series.

Lila Perl lives in Beechhurst, New York.